Contents

England	Wales	Scotland	Ireland	British settlers overseas	Total: 3.76 million
 2.25 million	0.21 million	0.5 million	0.8 million	None	

1500 Population estimates

England in about 1500

Our story continues in 1485 when a Welsh prince, Henry Tudor, became King Henry VII of England.

His titles were King of England, Lord of Ireland and Prince of Wales. He ruled over England, had some powers in Ireland and Wales but none in Scotland as the Scots had their own line of kings. At this time, the kingdoms of the British Isles – Scotland, Ireland, Wales and England – were not united.

Ireland

Ireland was divided into lordships. Some were ruled by descendants of the Norman-English barons who had conquered land from the time of William I. Others were ruled by Gaelic lords. Henry VII claimed lordship of Ireland but his power was confined to an area in and around Dublin (known as the Pale) and some English lordships beyond it.

Wales

Wales was divided into two regions. Lands conquered by Edward I were known as the Principality, and ruled by Henry VII as Prince of Wales. The rest were Marcher lordships, most ruled by the Crown and some by almost independent barons.

Were there different religions as well as different languages?

Scotland

Scotland had been ruled by the Stuart family since 1406, and James IV ruled from 1488.

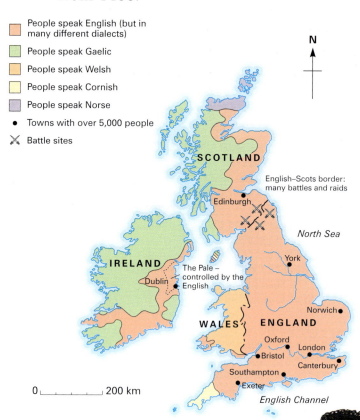

- People speak English (but in many different dialects)
- People speak Gaelic
- People speak Welsh
- People speak Cornish
- People speak Norse
- • Towns with over 5,000 people
- ✗ Battle sites

▲ The British Isles in about 1500

There was only one common religion: Christianity. The Pope in Rome was the head of the Christian Church – the Catholic one, that is.

In 1503 Henry VII linked the Tudor family of England to the Stuart family of Scotland by marrying his daughter Margaret to James IV. He also linked the Tudors to Europe by marrying his eldest son Arthur to Catherine of Aragon (Spain).

QUEST

The World of Enlightenment

Bea Stimpson

Stanley Thornes (Publishers) Ltd

First published in 1999 by:
Stanley Thornes (Publishers) Ltd
Ellenborough House
Wellington Street
CHELTENHAM GL50 1YW
England

00 01 02 03 / 10 9 8 7 6 5 4 3 2

A catalogue record for this book is available from the British Library.

ISBN 0-7487-3658-1

Designed and typeset by Clare Park

Illustrated by Francis Bacon, Beverly Curl, Hardlines and Angela Lumley

Cover artwork by Beverly Curl

Picture research by Simon Conti

Printed in Hong Kong by Wing King Tong

The author wishes to acknowledge Peter Burton and Melanie Gray of Stanley Thornes for their advice during the preparation of this book.

Thanks are owed to the illustrators for their skill and patience in producing the artwork. She also wishes to thank her teaching colleagues, Norman Hobson and Simon Rodden, for their practical suggestions.

She is particularly indebted to her husband, Michael, for the support he has given.

Acknowledgements

With thanks to the following for permission to reproduce photographs and illustrations:

Bibliothèque de Genève: 14(t)

Bodleian Library, Oxford: 27(m), 64(b)

Bridgeman Art Library: (Private Collection) 20(b), (Belvoir Castle) 46, (Prado, Madrid) 54(t), (Private Collection) 75, (Museum of London) 81(b), (Private Collection) 88, (Guildhall Library, Corporation of London) 90, (British Library) 104, (Kunsthistorisches Museum, Vienna) 19, 2(tl)

British Library Reproductions: 5(m), 34, 45, 59

The British Museum: 8(l, br)

Edinburgh University Library: 83(b)

The Fotomas Index: 7(tr), 30(both), 33(b), 48, 61(t), 65, 74(t), 76(br), 80, 98(both), 99, 102(t)

Getty Images: 58(b), 79(t), 105(b)

The Greenwich Foundation for the Royal Naval College: 103

Michael Holford Photographs: 82(b)

Ipswich Borough Council Museums and Galleries Collections: 24(b)

The Pepys Library, Magdalene College, Cambridge: 36(both)

Mary Evans Picture Library: 6(tr, bl), 9(b), 13(both), 14(b), 15, 21, 22(m), 31, 32, 35(b), 37(m), 42(b), 50, 51(t), 52, 53(both), 54, 55, 57(both), 58(t), 61(b), 66(both), 67(b), 68, 72, 73(b), 74(b), 76(l), 77, 78, 79(b), 83(t), 86(t), 89(b), 92(both), 94, 95 (t), 100(b),101, 105(t), 106

Museum of London: 84(t), 85(b), 87, 91

National Gallery, London: 51(b)

National Trust Photo Library: 29(b)

National Maritime Museum, London: 29(m), 38(b), 39, 42(t), 43, 44, 63

By Courtesy of the National Portrait Gallery, London: 8(tr), 16(both), 20(t), 22(tr, br), 24(m), 28(both), 37(m), 64(t), 67(t), 81(t), 82(t), 93, 100(t)

Public Record Office: 11(b)The Board of Trustees of the Armouries, 17(m)

The Royal Collection © Her Majesty The Queen: 17(b), 18, 22(bl), 62(both), 102(b)

Private Collection: 27(b)

Royal Commission on the Historical Monuments of England: 11(t)

By courtesy of The Duke of Rutland, Belvoir Estate: 10

Philip Sauvain Collection: 12, 73(t)

Skyscan: 23

Edwin Smith: 97

By kind permission of the Marquess of Tavistock and the Trustees of the Bedford Estate: 25

Wellcome Centre Medical Photographic Library: 95(b)

Every effort has been made to contact copyright holders and we apologise if any have been inadvertently overlooked.

rinting meant more hips could have opies of haps	An astrolabe helped to find position more exactly	Rudder to sail more accurately	Magnetic compass told sailors where north was	Triangular lateen sail to sail against the wind

ventions that helped sailors

The world in about 1500

If you look at this map, you can see what knowledge cartographers (map makers) had of the shape of the British Isles at that time.

The true size of the earth was not known and many Europeans still thought that it was as flat as a map. What Europeans did know was of the existence of countries in the East: Cathay (China), the Indies (India) and the Spice Islands (South-East Asia and Indonesia).

They desired the luxuries, spices, incense, silks and perfumes from these countries, but had to make long, hazardous journeys across the Mediterranean Sea and overland to buy them.

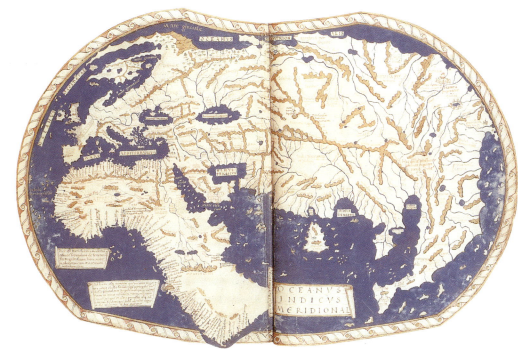

▲ Henricus Martellus's map of the world, drawn in about 1489

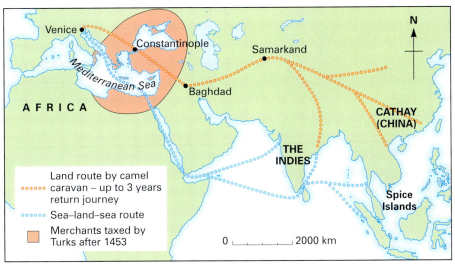

When the Turks captured Constantinople in 1453 and put taxes on goods passing through their lands, Europeans looked for alternative routes to the East.

▲ Land and sea routes were long and hazardous

If you look at Martellus's map, you can see how far Portuguese sailors had reached round the bottom of Africa in their search for a sea route to India, without falling off the edge of the world. Europeans who believed the world was round thought that if they sailed westwards across the Atlantic Ocean, it would be possible to reach China and India. What they did not know was of the existence of an unknown continent that lay between Europe and Asia.

Exploration

Was the unknown continent America?

Yes, though the sailor who discovered it, Christopher Columbus, thought he had landed on one of the islands east of Japan. He had actually landed in the West Indies.

▲ John Cabot

In 1497 John Cabot, an Italian sponsored by England, tried to reach Asia by sailing north-west. He found part of Canada – and cod.

John Cabot 1497

Columbus 1492
Columbus 1493
Columbus 1502
Columbus 1

▲ Christopher Columbus

In 1492 Christopher Columbus, an Italian sponsored by Spain, sailed westwards and landed on the island of San Salvador (Holy Saviour), now called Watling Island. He then visited Cuba and Haiti. He returned home with six Indians, a parrot, some fish – and gold. He died in 1506, not knowing that he had landed in America.

In 1494, because of the danger of trading wars between the two Christian nations Spain and Portugal, the Pope divided the world in two.

Spain could explore and conquer all the lands 320 leagues west of the Cape Verde Islands, while Portugal had power east of this line.

Pope divides the world 1494

Gold, ivory and cod

By 1477, skilful Portuguese sailors with superior ships had, over 60 years, discovered various places on the west coast of Africa.

In 1488, despite terrible storms, Bartholomew Diaz (Portuguese) rounded the southern tip of Africa without falling off the edge of the world.

▲ Vasco da Gama

In 1497 Vasco da Gama (Portuguese) followed Diaz's route, then sailed up the east African coast. With the help of a pilot given by the ruler of Malindi, he sailed across the Indian Ocean and dropped anchor at Calicut, India on May 20, 1498. When he sold his cargo of spices on his return to Portugal, it was for 60 times more than it had cost him in India!

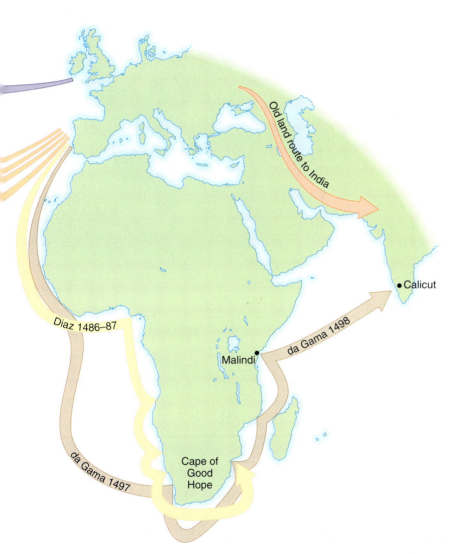

Old land route to India

Calicut

Diaz 1486–87

da Gama 1498

Malindi

da Gama 1497

Cape of Good Hope

▲ A modern map showing the routes taken by explorers, 1492–1498

The Portuguese could boast of cargoes of ivory and spices, and the Spanish could boast of finding gold. These two nations forged ahead in the race for colonies. The English, for the time being, had to be content with the useful but unglamorous cod.

|  Red and white rose |  Red dragon of Cadwaladr supported Henry's coat of arms. Used on banner at Bosworth to stress alleged descent from British kings. | English leopards | French lilies | Crown and thorn bush | Beaufort portcullis |

Tudor symbols and royal badges

THE FIRST TUDOR **2**

Henry VII

England in 1485 was a tiny kingdom in this vast world, but to Henry Tudor, a Welsh prince of the House of Lancaster, it was one worth fighting for. Henry had been plotting to win the English crown for 12 years and immediately after defeating Richard III, of the House of York, at Bosworth Field, he claimed the crown as his through the 'right judgement of God given in battle'.

Henry judged wisely when he married a possible rival, Elizabeth of York, daughter of Edward IV. By marrying Elizabeth, Henry united the warring families of Lancaster and York. The symbols of the red and white roses were joined to make one Tudor rose.

Henry used other symbols, such as the English leopards, French lilies, the Welsh dragon and the portcullis sign of his mother, Margaret Beaufort, to show his subjects the strength of the House of Tudor.

Henry recognised the importance of being seen to be King. He re-established kingship with all its pomp and pageantry. Although frugal in many ways, he spared no expense at court, where lavish banquets, processions, entertainments and tournaments were admired by foreign ambassadors. Even his dogs wore silk collars!

Henry was certainly held in awe by his subjects who bared their heads, bowed and genuflected as he walked past.

▲ Henry VII wearing a cloth of gold surcoat lined with white fur

▲ A gold medallion struck to commemorate Henry's marriage to Elizabeth of York in January 1486

▲ The medallion's reverse shows the joining of the red and white roses, a symbol of unity

Prince Arthur born (dies aged 15)	Princess Margaret born	Prince Henry born	Princess Elizabeth born (dies aged 3)	Princess Mary born	Prince Edmund born (dies aged 16 months)	Princess Katherine born (dies soon after her mother)	Queen Elizabeth dies a week after childbirth
1486 September 20	1489 November	1491 June 28	1492	1495 March	1499 February	1503 February 2	1503 February 9

New Learning

Margaret Beaufort had a strong religious influence on Henry, her only child. She used some of her personal wealth for educational purposes, such as founding a new college at Cambridge University, St John's, and refounding another, Christ's. These, and colleges at Oxford University, became centres for a New Learning which advanced religious and philosophical thought.

Henry welcomed scholars at court. These included Grocyn, who gave the first public lecture in Greek, and Linacre, a scholar of Greek as well as a personal physician to Henry.

Why did people study the ancient Greeks when we speak of the learning as being new?

Because scholars in Europe at this time found the ideas and writings of the Greeks and Romans, many of them who lived well before Christ, worth rediscovering.

They translated these works and made them available for others to study for the first time. Writers, scientists, mathematicians, architects and artists began to look again at all aspects of human life, and began to ask questions that challenged accepted beliefs.

This period of rediscovery became known as the Renaissance, or rebirth. Italy was the centre for this movement for much of this period, and Grocyn, Linacre and their friends studied there. They in turn influenced Henry, who began to follow the pattern of other European courts.

He built his own library and established poets, writers and artists at his palace in Richmond, London. This was decorated with tapestries and stained glass from Europe.

The scholars at court, and Oxford and Cambridge, became known and respected in Europe. Slowly but surely Henry's tiny kingdom was becoming a significant part of the known world.

▲ Erasmus, a famous scholar of the Renaissance

9

Yeoman then

Beefeater today

The businessman king

Was Henry VII a wealthy king?

He was by no means rich when he came to the throne and had to borrow money to pay off Crown debts. By 1492, however, he had paid off his debts and had begun to make a profit.

▲ Henry with his tax inspectors, Empson and Dudley

Kings were expected to 'live off their own', which meant running the country out of their own income. Henry kept a careful watch on his finances. Royal account books show that he signed every page. He raised his revenue from various sources:

- A parliamentary grant each year.
- Customs duties from wool.
- Trade treaties with foreign countries.
- Fees paid to him on the death of a lord or the marriage of the lord's children.
- Richer subjects were sometimes made to lend him money (forced loans) or give him money out of their love for him (benevolences)!
- Speedy payments from the Crown's debtors or fines.
- Heavy fines for lords breaking laws of maintenance (using force to settle a law suit).
- Nobles were prevented from keeping retainers (people in their service) other than servants. If these servants wore badges or uniform (livery), the lords were fined heavily.
- Two legal experts, Richard Empson and Edmund Dudley, helped him to extract more money from his nobles. Working within the law, but using informers, they clawed money back from the wealthy.

So, by keeping a tight rein on his finances and 'over-mighty subjects', Henry slowly but surely established a strong, stable kingdom.

500 in honour of the Trinity	2,500 in honour of the five wounds of Christ	2,500 in honour of the joys of Our Lady	450 in honour of the nine orders of angels	150 in honour of the patriarchs	600 in honour of the 12 apostles	2,300 'which maketh up the hool nombre in honour of all the saints'

Masses for the soul of Henry VII

Henry VII's will

Between 1502 and 1503, Henry's wife, Queen Elizabeth, and his eldest son, Arthur, both died. Henry, grief-stricken, gradually withdrew from court life. He seemed to prefer thinking about life after death rather than enjoying life here on earth in one of his magnificent residences.

In 1503 he ordered the building of a glorious Chantry Chapel inside Westminster Abbey.

Three royal tombs of marble were made by an Italian Renaissance sculptor, Pietro Torrigiano. Relics such as a piece of the 'true (crucifixion) cross', set in gold and jewelled, and a leg of St George, were displayed there. The Chapel was served by a separate body of priests. After Henry's death, the priests began a ceaseless chanting of prayers.

▲ Henry VII's chapel

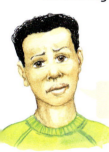

Why did they do this?

Because Catholics believed that the journey towards the light of God, which began at birth, did not end with death. People paid priests to say masses so that the souls of the dead could leave purgatory (a place between heaven and hell) and go to heaven.

In his will, Henry asked that silver statues of himself praying should be set up at three shrines.

He left bequests of money for the sick and needy, for monasteries and for the improvement of roads on which pilgrims might travel. He confessed his sins and unworthiness. He called on the Virgin Mary, the saints, the angels and the heavenly host and the faithful to pray for him.

He requested that 10,000 masses should be said for his soul by priests in all the London parish churches. Henry had many devoted priests. Other Catholics, however, felt their priests lacked devotion.

▲ Henry's will

'See a piece of the true cross here...  and here... and here... and here... and here... and here... and here... and here... and here... and here... and here... and here... and here...' There are enough pieces of the true cross to build a boat!

Criticism of relics

RELIGIOUS
3
DISCONTENT

Rumblings

Why did some Catholics feel priests lacked devotion to their work?

The Church had become unbelievably wealthy, but even the poorest peasants had to pay for its upkeep by giving one tenth of their earnings – a tithe – to the Church.

They also had to pay the priests for services such as burials or writing wills. So they complained when priests could not be bothered to walk a fair distance to hear a death-bed confession, or read services in Latin correctly. They were upset when priests, despite their vow of celibacy (no sexual relations), lived openly with women and had children. People saw churches and cathedrals with gold and silver candlesticks, crosses and chalices (drinking cups), beautiful paintings, sculptures and carvings. They saw little of the bishops, who rarely visited their dioceses, yet enjoyed the income they received.

Scholars such as Erasmus criticised the Church without wanting to destroy it. They wanted to preserve what was holy and reform what was unnecessary or corrupt.

One critic, an Italian friar, Savanarola, wrote that earlier, 'the chalices were made of wood, the bishops of gold'. Now 'the Church hath chalices of gold and bishops of wood'. Savonarola was later burnt as a heretic.

What is a heretic?

A person whose religious opinions are different from the accepted beliefs of the Church.

One courageous critic, who also risked death, dared to claim that the authority of the Bible was greater than that of the Pope. His name was Martin Luther.

▲ 'The Fortress of Faith' – Catholics defending their faith against heretics

No. 27: They preach Man, not God, who say that the soul flies out of purgatory as soon as the money rattles in the chest

No. 86: Why does not the Pope, whose riches are enormous, build the basilica of St Peter with his own money instead of taking it from poor believers?

The Ninety-Five Theses

Luther

Martin Luther, a German monk and priest, hated the greed, bribery and corruption he had observed in the Church. When he became a teacher at the University of Wittenburg in Germany, he told his students that all that was necessary to be a Christian was to believe truly in Jesus Christ. If people had complete faith, God would forgive their sins and they would find salvation.

People, he declared, would not wipe out their sins by going on pilgrimages, praying to saints or buying indulgences.

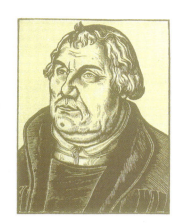

▲ Martin Luther

What were indulgences?

They were letters of pardon from the Pope who said that God would forgive the sins of anyone who paid money to the Church.

Pardoners travelled throughout Europe selling these confessional letters. In 1517 a friar, John Tetzel, came to Wittenburg selling indulgences. Half the money collected was to go towards building a new St Peter's Church in Rome. The other half was to pay off an Archbishop's debts. Luther was furious.

Luther wrote out a long list of arguments against such indulgences and nailed them to the church door at Wittenburg Castle. The list was later called the Ninety-Five Theses.

Although Luther did not realise it at the time, he had thus begun the Protestant Reformation. His ideas and beliefs were soon to attract thousands of followers.

In 1529 the word 'Protestant' came to be given to his followers. They did not want to destroy the Unity of Christendom. For Protestants, Christ had left one Church – theirs. For Catholics, Christ had left one Church – theirs.

From then on in Europe, there were two main forms of Christian worship: Protestant and Catholic.

▲ Selling indulgences – supervised by the Pope

13

John Calvin, founder of the Calvinist religious movement	Key belief was predestination	Strict rules, severe punishments	First offence: kiss the earth; last offence: pillory for one hour	First offence: fine; third offence: prison	For singing or dancing, anything immoral, dissolute or outrageous: prison for 3 days
1509–1564			Blasphemy	Drunkenness	Song and dance

Calvin and Knox

A Frenchman, John Calvin, was influenced by the works of Luther and became a devout Protestant and a leader of the Reformation.

▲ A 16th-century Calvinist temple in Lyon, France

What were his beliefs?

One main belief was known as predestination. He said that what people did on earth did not matter, as only those already chosen by God – the elect – would be saved.

He also argued that when the priest in Mass blessed the bread and wine, these things did not, as the Catholics believed, miraculously become the body and blood of Christ. They simply **represented** Christ's body and blood.

He believed in simple services. There were no crosses, candles or paintings of Jesus and the saints in Calvinist churches. The pastors (priests) preached and taught. The elders (presbyters) were allowed to enter people's homes to keep an eye on them. Pleasurable pastimes such as dancing and enjoying Christmas were frowned upon. Punishments for sinners were severe.

▲ John Knox

John Knox, a Scottish preacher, was influenced by Calvin when he visited him in Geneva and saw how he had reorganised the Church there. On his return to Scotland in 1559, he became the founder of the Presbyterian Church (Kirk). Knox, with his fiery personality and long black beard, was renowned for his preaching.

He persuaded the Scottish Parliament to accept the Reformed Faith as the official religion of Scotland, thus throwing out the Catholic version. Between 1559 and 1560, Catholics and Protestants struggled to gain power until the Reformists, the Protestants, won.

The Scots Confession, a statement of Protestant beliefs, became law in 1560.

	Folio size: 40 x 30 cm Quarto size (folio size folded in half): 30 x 20 cm Octavo size (folded again) came later: 20 x 15 cm	4d or 6d for a book: a day's wages for a craftsman	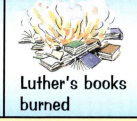 Luther's books burned	Pope rewards Henry VIII with title 'Defender of the Faith' ('Defensor Fidei') 
axton's ress at /estminster bbey				
476		1520	1521	Fid Def 2000

The power of print

Did Luther and Calvin ever visit England?

No, but what helped to spread their ideas was the invention of the printing-press. Printing transformed and opened up undreamed-of opportunities for people to learn.

It has been estimated that in 1450 there were only about 50,000 books in the whole Western world. By 1500 there were probably about nine million books in Europe alone.

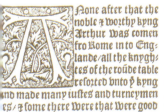

▲ A page from Mallory's *Morte d'Arthur*, printed at Westminster in 1529

In England, early books tended to be religious texts, school books and moral tales. Caxton, who introduced printing in England, even had a best-seller with his *Golden Legend* – stories about the saints, which went into seven editions. Then books on such studies as medicine, mathematics and astrology began to be published.

Pamphlets written by Luther and Calvin were imported or smuggled into England. This led to people being able to compare their religious beliefs with those of the humanists such as Erasmus. Then they could make up their own minds and have their own opinions.

What did humanists believe?

Instead of the Calvinist belief of predestination decided by God, humanists believed that human destiny was in the hands of individuals themselves.

The Church could not stop the flow of critical writings.

On May 12 1521 Luther's books were thrown by loyal Catholic churchmen into a bonfire in front of a crowd thought to be as many as 30,000 people.

Henry VIII, son of Henry VII, published a work condemning Luther, and the Pope rewarded him with the title 'Defender of the Faith'. England at this time was still a country of the one Catholic faith.

Birth of Thomas Wolsey, son of a butcher	Priest	Royal Chaplain	Henry VIII's almoner	Held several bishoprics; also Archbishop of York	Cardinal		Lord Chancellor	Pope's ambassador in England	Arrest and downfall	Dies before being tried for treason
1472	1498	1505	1509	1514	1515 September	December		1518	1529	1530

THE SECOND 4 **TUDOR**

Henry VIII

Henry VIII succeeded to the throne at the age of 17, and was generally acknowledged to be a magnificent 'Prince of the Renaissance'.

Why was he called that?

He seemed to offer so much promise. He had been surrounded by the best tutors; knew Latin, French and Greek; and could play several instruments and compose music.

He was an all-round sportsman, which promised well for someone who sought glory on the battlefield like his ancestors Henry V and the Black Prince. The popular Henry seemed to embody all the hopes of this exciting age of rediscovery.

Helping Henry to achieve glory was his chief minister, Cardinal Wolsey, who had risen swiftly to power through ability, ambition and loyalty to the King.

▲ Henry at the age of 20

Was he as popular as Henry?

Not at all! He was disliked by many for the way he flaunted his immense wealth and power.

He wore rich crimson-red robes, a sable scarf and a scarlet hat. Just as Christ was humble enough to ride on a donkey, Wolsey went to work on a mule! His beast, though, was bedecked with red velvet and gilt spurs! As he rode from Whitehall to Westminster, riders and footmen went before, carrying the Great Seal of England, his hat, two silver crucifixes, a silver pillar and four gilt pole-axes. Wolsey often carried an orange stuffed with a sponge of vinegar and herbs, as his visitors included the poor, many of whom stank.

Wolsey, like Henry VII's hated tax inspectors Empson and Dudley, was eventually to be charged with High Treason against his King. Other people during the next 37 years were to be similarly charged. There was only one sentence . . . death.

▲ Cardinal Wolsey

16

Army and navy

How could Henry seek glory on the battlefield when Henry VII left an actual army of only Yeomen of the Guard and 800 soldiers?

He built up a stock of modern weapons and developed his kingdom's defences first.

He amassed arms and made weapon-practice and archery compulsory for all able-bodied men. He added a Royal Guard to the Yeomen and employed expensive mercenary troops. He set up gun foundries, which made brass and iron guns, and established a royal armour factory at Greenwich.

He fortified the coast against French invasion by building castles of a new shape along the vulnerable south coast.

His father had left only six fighting ships, so, to strengthen his sea power, Henry established naval dockyards at Deptford and Woolwich near London; appointed a special board to run the navy; and eventually possessed the largest fleet outside the Mediterranean, with 90 warships of various sizes. His warship *Henri Grace à Dieu* had 184 guns. The ship was hardly used, but it impressed foreign visitors. On May 31 1520 Henry clambered on board the 'Great Harry' to sail to a very prestigious extravaganza indeed.

▲ A suit of armour made for Henry

▲ The *Henri Grace à Dieu* embarks from Dover for Calais

17

Battle of Spurs: Hapsburg Emperor Maximilian and Henry defeat French	Henry and Charles V allies against France	Holy League of Cognac included England against Charles V	Henry winched onto horse. Armour cut away from ulcerated leg for renewed war against France.	Peace with France. England keep Boulogne for 8 years.
1513 August 13	1522	1526	1544	1546

The Field of the Cloth of Gold

Firework dragon

Henry meets Francis at centre tent

Henry had 3,997 personal attendants; Wolsey had 12 chaplains, 50 gentlemen and 237 servants

Jousting area

Fountain spurting wine

▲ The Field of the Cloth of Gold

The 'Great Harry' brought Henry, his wife Catherine of Aragon and Cardinal Wolsey to Calais for diplomatic purposes. On June 7 1520 Henry met Francis I of France for the first time. Talks proposing goodwill and friendship were held nearby in a temporary town of tents and pavilions.

Why was it called the Field of the Cloth of Gold?

Because of the vast quantity of rich gold material needed to cover the tents and make costumes for both courts.

Was the expense justified?

Behind all the outward show, the atmosphere was tense at times.

Soldiers who had fought each other as enemies in war found it difficult to drink together as companions in peace. Local peasants, however, did not find drinking together a problem, especially when fountains spurted free malmsey (a strong, sweet wine) and claret (a rich, red wine).

Both kings were young and proud. On one occasion, Henry said to Francis, 'Come, you shall wrestle with me.' Francis did and threw the English king to the ground. It took several courtiers to hold Henry back once he regained his feet.

The diplomatic talks of friendship were rather like the buildings; a temporary front, a façade. Both before and after the talks had finished Henry met secretly with the Emperor Charles V, and by 1522 a treaty had been signed between them, making them allies against the French.

Henry's reign was in fact marked by various alliances and cross-alliances with European powers, arrangements which were soon conveniently forgotten.

Despite all his expenditure on warfare, Henry achieved little glory in battle.

Catherine of Aragon

▲ The young Catherine

Catherine must have found her visit to France rather sad. At 34 she had only one surviving child, Mary. At 20, Claude, the Queen of France had three children, including the Dauphin Francis, and was expecting another baby.

Henry had married Catherine, his brother Arthur's widow, in 1509, when he was 17. They had in fact been betrothed for seven years since the death of Arthur, and Henry genuinely desired the marriage. The connection with the prestigious Spanish court was also extremely desirable.

Catherine, who was deeply religious, considered herself during the betrothal already married in the eyes of God. Throughout their marriage she had, in many ways, proved to be an ideal queen and ambassadress for Henry. Well-educated, she was able to speak fluent classical Latin and, through study of the principles of the New Learning, tried to deepen her own religious understanding. The learned men at court – Erasmus, Linacre and More – respected her knowledge. Sadly, despite being utterly devoted to Henry (taking pride in embroidering his shirts and fussing over whether he had enough clean linen when abroad), Catherine was unable to bear a surviving son.

But she had a surviving daughter!

Yes, but Henry wanted a **male** heir to continue the Tudor dynasty.

In 1519 Catherine had to suffer the humiliation of watching the festivities for the birth of Henry's illegitimate son, Henry Fitzroy, by a mistress, Bessie Blount. This lady had been a maid of honour at court, as was another mistress, Mary Boleyn, whose wedding Catherine had attended. Mary had a younger sister called Anne.

Secret examination into first marriage: valid or not?	Wolsey fails to obtain divorce and falls from favour	Rise of minister Thomas Cromwell	Cromwell helps to bring English Church under Henry's control	Archbishop Cranmer declares first marriage invalid	Henry excommunicated by Pope
1527 May	1529 Autumn	1529	1531	1533 May	June

Anne Boleyn

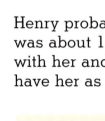

Henry probably met Anne Boleyn in 1526, when she was about 18 and Henry 35. He fell passionately in love with her and at a certain point decided that he would have her as his wife.

Was divorce easy to obtain then?

It was almost impossible as it was against the teachings of the Catholic Church.

▲ Anne Boleyn

Henry could only re-marry if the Pope agreed that his first marriage to Catherine should not have taken place. Henry convinced himself that in the eyes of God his marriage was not lawful. He had proof from the Bible, he believed, as the Book of Leviticus says: 'If a man shall take his brother's wife, it is an unclean thing: they shall be childless.' Henry interpreted 'childless' as meaning 'without a son'. Unfortunately for Henry, the Book of Deuteronomy says: 'Her husband's brother shall take her [the childless widow] to him as a wife.'

Catherine insisted that they were lawfully married and that they had a legitimate child, Mary, born in 1516.

So began, in 1527, a long and complicated case in which Henry tried every possible means to secure his divorce and be free to marry Anne Boleyn. The Pope, not wishing to offend Henry or Catherine's nephew, the powerful Emperor Charles V, could not reach a decision.

In 1531, however, Henry separated from Catherine. Then, in late 1532, Anne became pregnant, and in January 1533 she and Henry were secretly married. A new Archbishop of Canterbury, Thomas Cranmer, granted Henry his divorce and Anne was crowned queen on June 1.

▲ Henry in a characteristic aggressive pose

The Pope responded by excommunicating (expelling) Henry from the Catholic Church.

In September, Anne gave birth to a girl, Elizabeth.

The break with Rome

What did Henry do next?

In February 1534 he made his marriage to Anne legal by getting Parliament to pass an Act of Succession.

Then, in November 1534, Parliament passed an Act of Supremacy. 'The King, our sovereign Lord, his heirs and successors, shall be the only supreme head of the Church of England.' The Pope no longer had power over England's Church. Henry had it all. Anyone refusing to swear the oath of succession and denying that the King was head of the Church would suffer death.

Did anyone refuse to swear the oath?

About 80 people, including two highly respected men – Thomas More, Lord Chancellor, and Bishop Fisher – refused to swear an oath and believed that the Pope, not Henry, should be head of the Church. They were all executed.

▲ Henry crushes the Pope

Catherine, too, refused to swear the oath, but she was already ill and died in January 1536, devoted to Henry to the end. Henry and Anne wore yellow – the colour of rejoicing – the day after her death, but for Anne the joy was shortlived.

Her second pregnancy in 1534 had failed and Henry's attention had turned to another Lady of Court, Jane Seymour.

In January 1536 Anne miscarried of a male child. 'I see God will not give me male children,' muttered Henry ominously. Anne was never popular, but her end was swift and terrible. On May 2 1536 she was arrested on charges of adultery with five men, including her brother. The men were executed and Anne was beheaded on May 19. The following day, Henry and Jane Seymour were betrothed.

21

Four more wives

The perfect wife

▲ Jane Seymour (Protestant)

Henry was 45 when he married Jane Seymour (aged about 25) in 1536. England rejoiced when she gave birth to a son, Prince Edward. Henry is said to have wept when he took the baby in his arms. Twelve days after giving birth, however, Jane died of blood-poisoning.

The unwanted wife

The 24-year-old Anne of Cleves came from a Protestant area of the Lowland Rhine. Henry needed allies against Catholic France and Spain. Unfortunately, he was not attracted to Anne. Six months after marriage in January 1540, they were divorced.

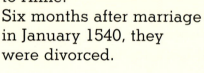

▲ Anne of Cleves (Protestant)

▲ Henry at the age of 53

The unfaithful wife

▲ Katherine Howard (Catholic)

Henry married the 19-year-old Katherine Howard when he was 48. By then he was grossly overweight, with ulcerated legs and thrombosis. After marriage, Katherine foolishly renewed a relationship with a former acquaintance. She was beheaded in February 1542.

The virtuous wife

Catherine Parr was widowed at 31. By this time (1543), Henry needed a nurse. Catherine's apothecaries' bills show stocks of olive-oil suppositories, plasters, sponges, liquorice and cinnamon comfits. Henry died on January 28 1547, aged 55.

▲ Catherine Parr (Protestant)

It took 16 tall and strong Yeomen of the Guard to lower Henry's coffin beside that of 'Our true and loving wife Queen Jane'.

Thomas Cromwell, Henry's chief minister, made Vicar-General of Church of England: he sent in lawyers to monasteries	How many attended divine service?	Did women visit the monastery by backways or otherwise?	Were meals over-rich?	Did the brothers dress extravagantly?

Questions put by lawyers

Dissolution of the monasteries

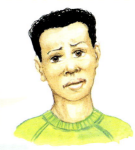

Why did Henry destroy the monasteries?

He needed the money: European rulers were angry at his treatment of Catherine of Aragon and the Pope and there was a risk of invasion.

Monasteries owned about a quarter of England's land, and the annual income from about 800 'houses' was more than the royal revenue. Teams of lawyers were sent in to ask questions. They found plenty of evidence to justify closure. Monks had wives and children, silver had been stolen, and lords had used monasteries as virtual hotels for months at a time.

In 1536 Parliament ordered the closure of 270 smaller 'houses'.

What was the result of this?

There were rebellions in Lincolnshire and in the north, where 53 houses had been closed.

One rebellion failed, but in Yorkshire a lawyer, Robert Aske, gathered 30,000 armed men at Doncaster. This rebellion, known as the Pilgrimage of Grace, was a serious threat to Henry, who made promises to the rebels which were never to be kept. Indeed the rising was crushed and over 200 people, including Aske, were executed.

By 1540 all the monasteries were closed and the land was sold off to the highest bidders. Most monks and nuns received pensions and all the moveable wealth, such as silver plate, went to the Treasury. Buildings decayed, libraries were broken up, shrines were destroyed, and the poor no longer received alms at the monastery gate.

Although the monasteries were ruined, Parliament kept the Catholic faith by passing the Statute of Six Articles. This retained all the Catholic beliefs and worship. Protestants called the Act 'the whip with six strings' because punishments for breaking the articles were severe. England was still a Catholic country.

▲ Fountains Abbey in Yorkshire as it looks today

23

Edward VI crowned	Dissolution of chantries	Royal injunctions ordered weekly sermons. Relics and images were removed.	New Book of Common Prayer written by Cranmer	Second prayer book written by Cranmer	42 Articles	Death of Edward VI
1547 February 19	1547	1547	1549	1552	1553 June	July 6

THE THIRD AND FOURTH TUDORS

5 Edward VI

Did Henry VIII die a Catholic?

Yes, but in this painting you can see that he is pointing out his son, Edward – who was a Protestant – to be his successor. The Pope is being crushed underfoot again. Next to Edward is the Protestant Duke of Somerset.

▲ Henry VIII on his deathbed

Somerset, and later the Protestant Earl of Warwick, ruled as Lord Protectors on Edward's behalf, as he was only nine years old at his succession. Not surprisingly, then, Protestant reforms were soon in place.

In 1547, within a few months of Henry's death, the Six Articles of Catholic beliefs and worship were cancelled.

Chantry chapels were closed. Protestants did not believe in purgatory, so masses for the souls of the dead were not needed.

Laws declared that Catholic images such as sculptures and carvings should be destroyed or defaced. Shrines were demolished, and statues and wall-paintings were white-washed or mutilated.

In 1549 Archbishop Cranmer's first prayer book translated Latin services into English. Protests over changes led to rebellions, which were suppressed by the army.

In 1552 Cranmer's second prayer book went further. He left out the Mass and replaced it with Communion. In this service, the bread and wine represented Christ in spirit rather than actually becoming the body and blood of Christ, as Catholics traditionally believed.

Stone altars were replaced by wooden communion tables, and priests were ordered to wear simple white linen garments called surplices.

In 1553 all the teachings of the reformed Church were written down in 42 Articles.

When Edward died in 1553, aged 16, England was firmly Protestant. However, Edward's successor, his step-sister Mary, was firmly Catholic.

▲ A restored wall-painting: marks of mutilation from 1547 can still be seen

24

Mary I

Edward's step-sister, Mary, was like her mother, Catherine of Aragon: devoted to the Catholic faith. She was proud to be half-Spanish. These two loyalties were to make her extremely unpopular with her English subjects.

Her first Parliament in October 1553 abolished all the religious laws passed during Edward's reign. Mary wanted to return England to the Catholic faith.

But England by now had many Protestants who did not want to return to the Catholic faith. Mary genuinely believed that it was better for these Protestant heretics to die rather than to live in mortal sin. In the course of three years, nearly 300 Protestants died at the stake for their beliefs. Important bishops such as Cranmer were burned, but what upset onlookers most were the deaths of ordinary people such as craftsmen, widows and shopkeepers. One young mother gave birth while dying, but lived long enough to see her child thrown into the flames. These 'Marian' persecutions earned Mary the nickname 'Bloody Mary'.

On top of all this, Mary lost the support of her subjects by marrying the Catholic Prince Philip of Spain in 1554. When he became King of Spain in 1556, he persuaded Mary to join him in war against France. In 1558 this led to the loss of Calais, the last bit of French land held by the English. In the same year, Mary died.

She had failed to choose her advisers well or to understand the feelings of her subjects. Her step-sister, Elizabeth, daughter of Anne Boleyn, was to choose *her* advisers well and understand her subjects very well indeed.

▲ Philip and Mary

New Act of Supremacy: Elizabeth made Supreme Governor of Realm and Church of England	Prerogative powers: royal authority independent of Parliament	Issued proclamations: orders without advice of Privy Council. These had force of law but could not have people killed or property removed.

1558 Elizabeth's powers

THE FIFTH 6 TUDOR

Elizabeth I

The Protestant Elizabeth was 25 when she succeeded to the throne. She was disadvantaged as she was not very rich, was female – and unmarried. But her reign was to last for 44 years.

During this time she was responsible for governing her realm. In the 16th century monarchs were expected to make laws, keep law and order, make sure justice was seen to be done and defend the realm from attack. To help her do this, Elizabeth took advice from Parliament, Privy Councillors and courtiers. She needed the agreement of Parliament to raise money by taxation and to make new laws.

New laws were often suggested by her small group of advisers, the Privy Council. These men, serving under Elizabeth, were the centre of her government.

What did the Privy Councillors do?

They had two main functions.

One was to advise the Queen on important matters such as going to war (Elizabeth did not always take their advice). The other was to run the country. They met several times a week.

In any one morning session they might:

- deal with a quarrel between a Portuguese and an English merchant.

- arrange for two murder suspects to go on trial.

- organise 200 troops to go to Ireland.

- consider a charge that someone had used rude and obscene words.

- listen to a French ambassador complaining about English ill-treatment of French sailors.

- send orders for musters (military training) to Worcestershire. Orders for musters were given to Lord Lieutenants to carry out.

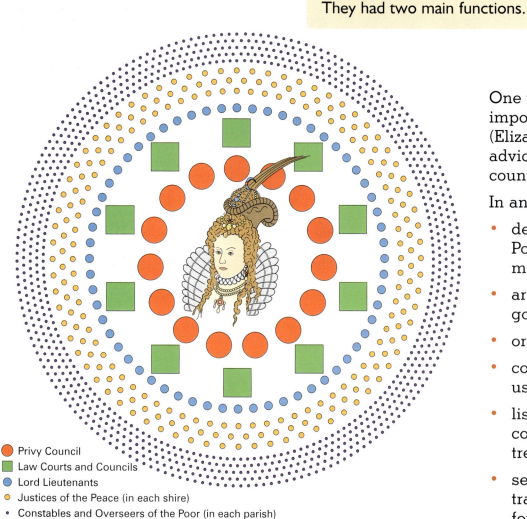

- 🔴 Privy Council
- 🟩 Law Courts and Councils
- 🔵 Lord Lieutenants
- 🟡 Justices of the Peace (in each shire)
- • Constables and Overseers of the Poor (in each parish)

▲ Elizabeth's government

Small and efficient; average 13 members	17 Lord Lieutenants in charge of 29 counties	Justices of the Peace: on average fewer than 10 per shire	Justices of the Peace: 40–50 per shire	Derbyshire: winter sessions – 18 out of 65 hanged; summer sessions – 12 out of 45 hanged
rivy Council **1595**	**1500**		**1580**	**1598** Quarter sessions

Elizabeth's government

Lord Lieutenants, who were often Privy Councillors, governed areas of the country. England had no professional army then, so one of their duties was to gather together (muster) all able-bodied men aged between 16 and 60 in each of their areas for military training each summer.

Other duties included collecting loans for the Privy Council, making sure no meat was eaten during Lent and on fish days, and checking on people who did not attend church, as such offenders could be fined. Lord Lieutenants had one deputy in each shire or county to help carry out their duties.

Also in each county, helping to keep law and order, were sheriffs and Justices of the Peace (JPs). The work of JPs gradually took over the work of sheriffs. They were appointed from local landowners and, though unpaid, the post carried some social prestige. Their administrative duties included writing references for servants and checking hospital accounts.

They saw that justice was done by holding Quarter Sessions every three months to try convicted criminals. Serious cases were passed over to the Assizes. These were held twice a year and presided over by one of 12 travelling judges from Westminster. JPs also had to appoint four Overseers of the Poor in each parish to organise poor relief. They made sure that the one constable in each parish carried out duties which included whipping beggars and arresting criminals.

▲ A travelling judge

Did Elizabeth ever visit her counties?

She realised the importance of being seen by her subjects and travelled on 'progresses' as far north as Norfolk.

During these progresses she was accompanied by her favourite courtiers. They made a splendid sight, as you can see here.

▲ Elizabeth in 1600

27

Fashions 'farre fetched deere bought'	Velvets from Genoa. Satins from Lucca and Cyprus.	Tafetta from Spain. Fustians from Milan. Worsteds from Norwich.	Goose-turd green. Pease-porridge tawny. Popinjay blue.	Maiden's blush (pink). Lustie gallant (vivid red).
	Influence of trade		Bold new colours	

The English Renaissance

Elizabeth always looked splendid. For her coronation on January 15 1559 she wore a cloth-of-gold mantle and kirtle (skirt and bodice) and a gold crown set with gems. She continued to look resplendent and regal during her long reign of 44 years. She played the part of Tudor monarch to perfection.

Elizabeth became queen just at a time when fresh interest was being shown in the theatre, plays, poetry, music, paintings and architecture.

London was the focus for this re-birth of interest in England, and these exciting times became known as the English Renaissance.

How do historians know these were exciting times?

Because of the wealth of writing, music, art and buildings that are still in existence today.

▲ Elizabeth I in her coronation robes

Even clothes worn by the rich are evidence of the confidence the English had in themselves. Social status was displayed in fashions of individual and dramatic style. Courtiers outdid each other in dress to gain the Queen's favour. This portrait of one of Elizabeth's favourites, Robert Dudley, shows the attention paid to the detail of his finery.

Bonnet with a jewelled band and ostrich feather

Long, pointed beard set off with moustache

Sir Robert wears the lesser George – a pendant on a chain showing he is a Knight of the Order of the Garter

Trunk hose embroidered with gold braid. Brocade between the panes.

▲ Sir Robert Dudley, Earl of Leicester

Doublet with a standing collar edged with a piccadill (stiffened with wire) border

Figure-of-eight ruff

Doublet slashed and pinked (small holes)

Buttons down front to a slight peascod belly (pointed down at the front)

Matching sleeves embroidered in gold braid

starch introduced in 1560s. ruffs were starched, damp nen dried over heated ticks.	Double-layered	Figure-of-eight	Cutwork	Cartwheel	Circular	Open ruff
uffs get bolder	1569	1575	1585	1587	1588	1598

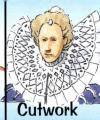

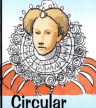
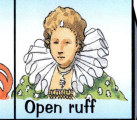

Rich man

This portrait shows George Clifford, third Earl of Cumberland, who was appointed the Queen's Champion of the Tilt in 1590. It was painted by Nicholas Hilliard, a celebrated artist of the time, who specialised in miniatures.

Some of the clothes seem rather like extraordinary fancy dress.

Yes, you are likely to think that!

You can see that Clifford's gauntlet has been thrown down ready to challenge, as if he were about to take on an opponent.

His bonnet is decorated with ostrich feathers. The Queen's glove, attached to the brim, is embroidered with the same pattern as the sleeves.

Across his surcoat is a gold belt and a sword. He holds a lance. His gauntlets match his helmet.

He has long, wavy hair and a pickdevant (short and pointed) beard with brushed-up moustache.

The wide, short sleeves are turned back to reveal white satin lining embroidered with celestial spheres and branches of olive.

The surcoat has a square-cut neckline, peascod belly and knee-length skirt. The skirt is ornamented with lines of jewels.

He certainly looks dressed to kill!

▲ George Clifford, Queen's Champion of the Tilt

His clothes were designed to impress, and they have certainly succeeded.

The homes of rich Elizabethans were impressive too. Again, the emphasis was on individuality and social status.

The contrast between rich and poor was striking.

▲ Hardwick Hall, Derbyshire, was built by the Countess of Shrewsbury in 1597

Hark, hark, the dogs do bark,
The beggars are coming to town.
Some in rags, and some in tags,
And some in silken gowns.

Poor man

Were there many poor people in Elizabethan times?

Yes, and the numbers had grown because of various changes in society during Tudor times.

For example, since the time of Henry VII, the great barons were no longer allowed to keep a huge number of private soldiers.

Also, since the time of Henry VIII, when monasteries were closed, the poor could no longer receive alms from the monks at the monastery gate.

▲ The contrast between a rich man and a beggar, 1569

Wages had risen but food prices had risen twice as fast. A depression in the wool trade meant that many weavers and spinners lost their jobs.

Labourers suffered too. Landowners preferred to keep sheep rather than let land to tenants. They fenced off (or 'enclosed') land on common ground for their flocks. Labourers and their families were turned away to fend for themselves.

All this led to an increase in the number of wandering homeless. These beggars were a mixture of honest men, women and children, rogues and vagabonds, discharged soldiers, the old and the sick.

How were these unemployed people treated?

▲ A whipping punishment of 1577

If you were considered to be an able-bodied wanderer, you were classed as a vagrant. Even genuine wanderers, such as pedlars, actors, minstrels and jugglers, were labelled as vagrants.

Punishments for begging were severe. In 1572 an Act of Parliament was passed which meant that punishment for a first offence was to be whipped and to have a $2\frac{1}{2}$ cm hole bored in the ear. A second offence meant whipping and boring of the other ear. A third offence meant death.

The same Act **did** order each district to provide money for the poor, but nothing was done to help the genuine unemployed who could not find work.

Act for Punishment of Rogues, Vagabonds and Sturdy Beggars: whipped until bloody, returned to own parish, put in jail, later found work.	Act for Relief of the Poor: churchwardens to collect fair poor rate from landowners. Money used for disabled, aged, poor and materials to provide work.	The Poor Law
1597	1598	1601

Beggar man, thief

How could you tell who the genuine unemployed were?

It was impossible to tell the real beggar from the false. Some would wear fake blood-stained bandages or deliberately make sores on their bodies. Even children were maimed in order to gain sympathy and money.

▲ Different kinds of beggars

The government became worried at the large numbers of 'sturdy' beggars who refused to work. Some of these organised themselves into bands of criminals who terrorised isolated farmhouses and villages.

Thomas Harman wrote down a list of the different types of criminal roaming the countryside at that time:

Hooker or angler	Thieves who hook clothes and goods from windows with long poles
Drunken tinkers	Thieves pretending to be tinkers
Counterfeit cranks	Beggars pretending to have fits by foaming at the mouth
Rufflers	Ex-soldiers or ex-servants who beg or rob
Dummerer	Beggars pretending to be dumb
Rogues	Beggars pretending to look for relations in a town to see who is worth robbing
Priggers of prancers	Horse stealers
Upright men	Leaders of bands of criminals
Kinching morts	Young female rogues

Gradually it became clear that many wanderers genuinely wanted work, and a change in approach to treating them fairly showed in the various poor laws passed by Parliament. Each parish became responsible for its own paupers, and relief centred round helping the poor in their own homes. Justices of the Peace monitored local systems of relief, and Overseers of the Poor were appointed annually to provide relief.

The Poor Law of 1601 reinforced all these practices and lasted for over 200 years.

31

Children of St Paul's act in front of Queen	Schools and universities encourage performances	Acte for Punishment of Vacobondes. Players to wear badge of lord.	'The Theatre', Shoreditch	'The Curtain'	Master of Revels at Court given official status and budget	Queen's company formed	'The Rose', Southwark
1560s		1572	1576	1577	1578	1583	1587

London theatre

Were all actors regarded as vagrants?

Actors were often regarded as no better than vagabonds. As plays were held in inn-yards, audiences were often rowdy.

Lord mayors and puritans disliked the theatre as they thought it led people to idleness and sin. As the Protestant faith became established, people lost interest in the traditional 'miracle' and 'mystery' plays performed by merchant guilds. Touring companies of professional 'players' became more popular. In 1572 an Act of Parliament gave players more status and protection: each was required to wear a badge to show who his lord and patron was.

Elizabeth enjoyed the theatre, and her patronage helped it to become accepted as a respectable pastime. After 1578, when her Master of Revels at Court was given a budget, he hired the touring companies with their cheaper, ready-made plays.

When and where were theatres built?

The first permanent theatre was built in 1576 by an actor, James Burbage. It was built in Shoreditch, north of the city of London, as lord mayors had always resisted any theatre-building inside the city walls. When this theatre made a profit, others were built outside the walls.

- Theatres built like inn-yards
- Open to sky for good lighting
- Tickets:
  1d – pit
  2d – galleries
  3d – best seats with cushions
- Food and drink brought round during performance

▲ The Swan Theatre in 1596

Flying flag, blowing trumpet and firing cannon announced start of play

Trumpeters' gallery

Roof called 'Shadow' or 'Heavens', often painted with sun, moon and stars

Little scenery

No actresses (all parts played by men and boys)

High stages, actors hid underneath

By the time William Shakespeare arrived in London in the 1580s, theatres were challenging churches as places to meet.

William Shakespeare

Shakespeare came to London as an actor. He later appeared in his own plays and it was as a playwright that he was best known, as he still is today.

What sort of plays did he write?

Wonderful and wordy ones!

▲ An engraving of William Shakespeare

Elizabethans loved being dramatic. Actors spoke out to address the audience and accompanied the words with bold actions such as stamping of feet and slapping of thighs. They used standard gestures to show emotions such as anger or fear. A textbook of the time lists a hundred ways to use the hands. Thieving, for example, was always done with the left hand. Shakespeare knew his audience. He understood human nature and the emotions such as love, desire, hate and despair we all experience in life.

In Elizabeth's reign, audiences were proud to be English.

In *Richard II*, Shakespeare wrote:

'This royal throne of Kings, this sceptr'd isle...

This precious stone set in a silver sea...

This blessed plot, this earth, this realm, this England.'

He could be delightfully rude and bawdy when appropriate, and at other times his words had a poetic quality. Like the best music, the beauty of his words touches the listener with its breathtaking perfection. Shakespeare was a genius. As Ben Jonson wrote, 'He was not of an age but for all time.'

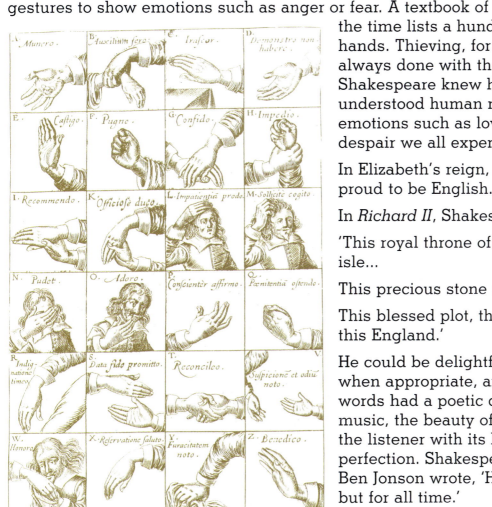

▲ Stylised gestures used by actors in the 17th century

33

Professional musicians formed Company of Waits. Performed 'official' music for City of London.	Gave first regular public concerts in England	Kettle drum, trumpets, organs, mandolins, sackbuts, hautboys, virginals, orpharion, pandoras, lute, viols, flutes, violins, cittern, recordes, cornetts, bandora
1570s		Elizabethan instruments

Music

Did theatres use music?

Yes, a great deal. They offered employment to professional musicians. London was not only the place where music was printed, it was also the place where the best variety of music could be heard.

Queen Elizabeth, like her father Henry VIII and grandfather Henry VII, was musical. Music was part of her daily life. She was a Protestant, but her church music was an important part of elaborate ceremonies and rituals more often associated with Catholic services.

Visiting ambassadors commented on the quality and beauty of the music they heard at the English court.

They would have listened to the choir of the Chapel Royal, which had the pick of the best voices in England. The 32 gentlemen and 12 boys of the Chapel set the standards of excellent musicianship.

▲ Miniatures from a manuscript showing children and gentlemen of the Chapel Royal in the funeral procession of Elizabeth I

What sort of music did they sing?

Chants, hymns, tunes and anthems. Two outstanding musicians and composers, Thomas Tallis and William Byrd, whose music is still played today, wrote for them.

I thought Protestants frowned on music of any kind?

Yes, they did, and in the parish churches of London and the country, organs were neglected, choirs disbanded, and books of music lost forever.

Protestants must have disapproved of Elizabeth's love of dancing too. She kept about 30 musicians, some of whom were foreign, to accompany the dances, and in old age she danced as a special mark of favour. Even in 1589, when she was 56 years old, a note recorded that the 'Q is so well, as I assure you, six or seven gallyards in a mornynge, besydes musycke and synginge, is her ordinary exercise.'

Spain colonises Antilles, north coast of South America, Panama, Jamaica, Puerto Rico, Cuba	Spain colonises Panama City, Spanish America, Aztec Mexico (Cortés), Chile, Ecuador, central America, central Colombia, Peru	Spain colonises Florida, West and Central Venezuela, north-west Argentina	Plantations and mines need slaves
1492–1519	1519–1550	1550s–1560s	

The English and the slave trade

Why did the English become involved in the slave trade?

Because it was so profitable. Spanish settlers in the West Indies and South America needed labour for their plantations and silver mines.

John Hawkins, a sailor, bought black slaves cheaply from African chiefs and sold them for huge profits to the Spanish.

After voyages in 1562 and 1564, he was so successful that Elizabeth allowed him to add a special crest, a picture of a black slave, to his coat of arms.

How dreadful! Surely Hawkins knew the slaves would be cruelly treated?

Indeed he did, but in the 16th century people were often indifferent to violence and brutality.

▲ Hawkins's coat of arms

Europeans considered themselves the 'masters' and exploited the inhabitants of the lands they conquered. In fact, nothing in the Bible condemned slave-handling. People believed Africans were black because of sins committed by their ancestors. The colour black was associated with evil and hell. Those born with a black skin were considered inferior beings. It is not surprising, then, that men, women and children were kept like animals in unspeakable conditions on board the slave ships and after landing.

In 1567, on a third voyage, Hawkins took one of his cousins, Francis Drake. They captured 500 slaves off the Guinea coast of West Africa and sold them to the Spanish. On their return, they stopped at a Mexican port for repairs after storm damage. Whilst there, they were ambushed by a Spanish fleet entering the harbour. Out of six English ships, only two escaped. Hawkins and Drake never forgave what they saw as Spanish treachery.

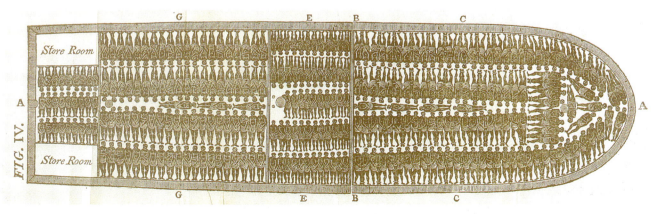

▲ Slaves packed into a ship. An 18th-century illustration.

Hawkins busy for 10 years building and repairing the Queen's fleet	He sometimes cut ships in half and inserted new sections	Lower ships lay snug in the water and were easier to manage. Larger ships carried more cannon.

1570s

John Hawkins

Why were Hawkins and Drake ambushed by the Spanish?

King Philip II of Spain had forbidden any foreign ship to enter Spanish ports. It may also have been because Hawkins and Drake were known pirates, raiding Spanish treasure ships for valuable cargo.

After the attack in Mexico, Hawkins was able to seek his own revenge on Philip. He became Comptroller of the Queen's navy and built 20 new ships. These were faster, lower and longer. They had bigger guns than any Spanish vessels.

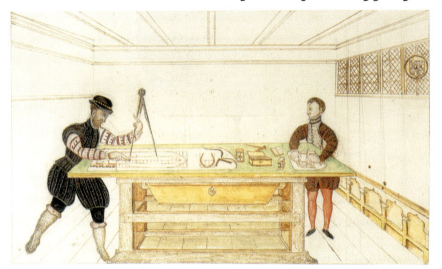

▲ Tudor shipwrights designing a galleon in 1586

Why did he build 20 new ships?

Philip at this time was immensely powerful. He ruled not only Spain, the principal Catholic country in the world, but most of the Netherlands, Belgium, Flanders, Sicily and two kingdoms of Italy.

He had hoped to extend his power to England when he married Mary Tudor, a Catholic. After her death, he was certainly unhappy at the Protestant rule of Elizabeth.

In 1587, when Elizabeth's cousin Mary Queen of Scots (a Catholic) was executed, he wanted, with the help of France, to mount a religious war against England.

He was also angry at Elizabeth's support of a rebel group of Dutch Protestants in the north of the Netherlands. These rebels had won some form of independence and Philip was hoping, with the help of his nephew, the Duke of Parma, to finish off the rebellion. Elizabeth was sympathetic to the rebels, and the Treaty of Nonsuch in 1585 gave them financial and military support. Philip decided to invade England, crush the Dutch rebels and triumph over northern Europe. He thus began to prepare an invasion fleet.

▲ Shipwrights copied the lines of a fish

	Only the Golden Hind rounds Magellan's Strait to enter Pacific Ocean	Reaches California. Returns across Pacific Ocean.	Lands on Spice Islands. Cloves taken on board.	Sails across Indian Ocean. Rounds Cape of Good Hope. Enters Atlantic Ocean. Returns to Plymouth.
ships ail				

577 Drake sails round the world   **1580** September

Sir Francis Drake

After the attack in Mexico, Drake's revenge against Philip took a more personal form than that of Hawkins.

How could an ordinary sailor conduct a personal campaign?

Drake was far from ordinary! He became known as the master pirate of the known world, and with good reason.

His revenge took the form of plundering Spanish settlements and treasure ships. In 1570 he raided towns in the West Indies. In 1577 he began an epic voyage which took him round the world and allowed him to bring back £2 million worth of treasure. Some of this came from the capture of Spain's richest treasure ship, the *Cacafuego*.

Elizabeth, on his return, received five packhorses laden with gifts such as emeralds, diamonds, cloth of gold and silver tableware.

Philip was furious and demanded that 'El Draque' be hanged as a pirate. Elizabeth, however, went on board the *Golden Hind* and knighted Drake with a sword.

English privateers (or 'private adventurers') carried on plundering. Although such piracy was never officially recognised by the government, it became an almost respectable profession.

▲ The *Golden Hind* captures the *Cacafuego*, 1579

How could Elizabeth approve of this?

She was not a wealthy monarch. As long as sailors could be disowned if things went wrong, Elizabeth was happy to share the spoils of pirating.

She would assure the Spanish ambassador of her disapproval of these pirates, yet at the same time wear silk dresses made out of sumptuous plundered silks. Despite the profits from raids at sea, England was still poorer and weaker than Spain, and so Elizabeth was anxious to avoid war.

▲ Sir Francis Drake, the master pirate of the known world

Singeing the King of Spain's beard

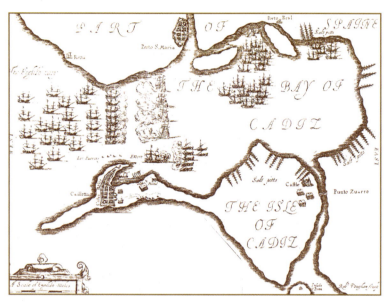

▲ The raid at Cadiz harbour

Did Elizabeth stop Drake from pirating the seas?

No. She angered Philip even further when she allowed Drake to rob Spanish settlements in 1585.

In 1587, Drake sailed on his cheekiest and most daring raid. He attacked ships being assembled for the invasion of England in Cadiz harbour. It was so successful it delayed the departure of the invasion fleet for over a year. Drake was able to boast colourfully that he had 'singed the King of Spain's beard'.

As tension between Elizabeth and Philip grew, Elizabeth tried to avoid war through negotiation and compromise. Her advisers met with the Duke of Parma, who was based in the Netherlands. The Duke preferred a compromise, but Philip demanded victory by battle at sea.

Philip wanted English Catholics to be tolerated, no more help to be given to the Dutch rebels and for England to pay for the full cost of an invasion – an extraordinary demand! He knew that England had no professional army to defend the country. If he could land his troops on English soil he was sure Elizabeth would agree to more terms. But first he had to get his troops across the sea.

Was this a problem?

Philip's military power was great, but until he conquered Portugal in 1580, he had no proper ocean-going navy at all.

He needed to strengthen his fleet by chartering ships from other European nations. Agents were sent to Germany and Italy to buy cannon, gunpowder and all the weapons of war. Organising the Armada was a colossal task, but by the spring of 1588 Philip's invasion fleet was ready.

▲ King Philip II of Spain

| fleet's banner blessed in Lisbon Cathedral | Philip II shaves his head like a monk and prays constantly | Ships had names of saints: San Felipe, Santa Maria de Vison, San Juan de Portugal | Every soldier, sailor, officer and slave confessed his sins before sailing | The Armada leaves Corunna for England |

588 April 25   July 2

The Spanish fleet

What did the Armada look like in 1588?

Formidable. There were 130 ships, divided into 10 squadrons.

Three main types of ships made up the fleet:

- 24 Portuguese and Spanish galleons were the front-line fighting ships. They carried the heaviest guns and were rather like floating castles.

- 41 merchant ships from all over Europe were converted for battle.

- 4 galleasses and 4 galleys made up the fighting ships.

Galleasses used both oars and sails to drive them through the water. The Armada also needed a squadron of 23 supply ships, called urcas or hulks.

▲ The Armada

Two were hospital ships, others carried horses and mules, and some carried land battle and ship repair equipment. Five thousand extra pairs of shoes and 11,000 pairs of sandals were also taken.

Food supplies were needed for 30,000 men. These included 600,000 pounds of salt pork, 40,000 gallons of olive oil and 14,000 barrels of wine, as well as biscuits, fish, rice, cheese and water. Of the men, 18,937 were soldiers, 8,050 sailors, six surgeons, six physicians, 180 priests, 50 administrators and 146 young gallants (merchant adventurers) who took 728 servants.

How do we know such precise figures?

The Spanish government deliberately published the information and distributed it throughout Europe. It was probably to frighten the English in advance.

The Commander of the Fleet was the Duke of Medina Sidonia. He was a brilliant administrator, but had no experience of sea or war. He wrote, 'My health is not equal to such a voyage, for I know by experience of the little I have been at sea that I am always seasick and always catch cold.'

A seasick naval commander!

39

	Deal Castle restored	Castles, forts and blockhouses of Henry VIII's time restored. Renewed defences on Isle of Wight and Southampton. Dover pier restored.	Ships' names included Dreadnought, Swiftsure, the Revenge, Tiger and Triumph	130 ships based at Plymouth

1588 Defences stepped up   **1588**

The English fleet

What did the English fleet look like in 1588?

It too had about 130 ships, 60 of which were fighting ships. English ships were smaller. A Spanish galleass could be 50 metres long, about the length of six buses. An English galleon would be about half that length.

Captain's cabin with glass windows, damask curtains and wood panelling to keep out mice

Capstan to raise and lower the anchor

Pumps

Store for anchor cables

Gun deck where the crew ate and slept. Fleas and lice infected clothes.

Captain's gallery

Officers' quarters

Whipstaff to move the rudder

Food store in hold

Rats, mice and worms

Cookroom

Sick and wounded men

Ballast to steady the ship

Food store

Ammunition store

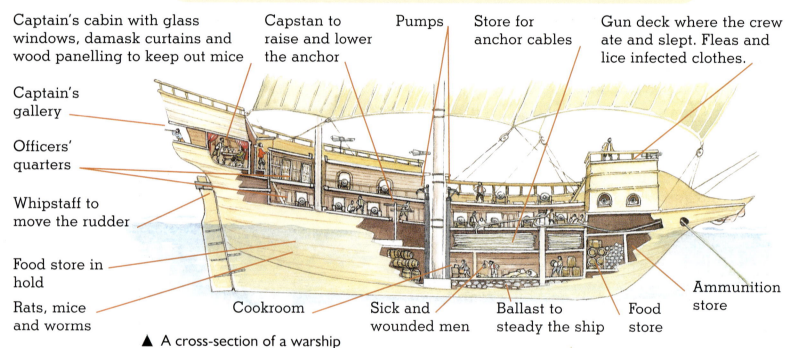

▲ A cross-section of a warship

Hawkins's ships were specially designed for Francis Drake's new type of sea battle. Instead of trying to get soldiers on board enemy ships for hand-to-hand fighting, sailors were trained to handle the new ships expertly, using long-range guns. He cut down the high castles and made ships longer to carry more guns. In speed and armaments, England had the advantage.

Many smaller ships, including pinnaces for scouting, were built on the same lines. They were armed and accustomed to fighting. Most seamen came from London, but many other ports contributed ships and men.

Was Drake the Commander of the Fleet?

No, because in the 16th century it was the custom for the aristocracy, noblemen by birth, to command.

The Commander was Elizabeth's cousin, Lord Howard of Effingham, whose father, two uncles and great grandfather had been Lords Admirals of the Fleet. He wrote, 'I would rather live in the company of these noble ships than in any other place.' He wisely appointed Drake, the popular hero, as Vice-Admiral.

The Armada: July 29 to August 9 1588

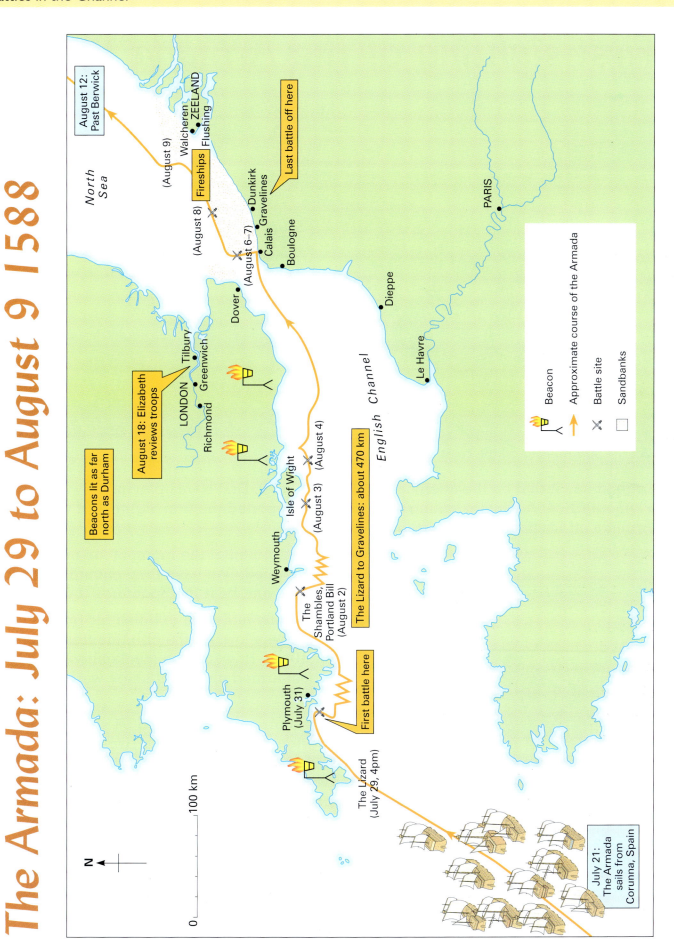

August 12: Past Berwick

ZEELAND
Walcheren
Flushing

(August 9)

North Sea

Last battle off here

Fireships (August 8)

Dunkirk
Calais
Gravelines
(August 6–7)
Boulogne

PARIS

Dover

Dieppe

English Channel

Le Havre

August 18: Elizabeth reviews troops

Tilbury
LONDON
Greenwich
Richmond

Beacons lit as far north as Durham

Isle of Wight
(August 4)
(August 3)

The Lizard to Gravelines: about 470 km

Weymouth

The Shambles, Portland Bill (August 2)

First battle here

Plymouth (July 31)

The Lizard (July 29, 4pm)

July 21: The Armada sails from Corunna, Spain

Legend:
- Beacon
- Approximate course of the Armada
- ✗ Battle site
- ☐ Sandbanks

N

100 km

0

41

Spanish gun carriages with 2 wheels. Difficult to move and aim.

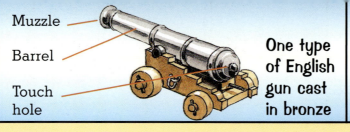
Muzzle

Barrel

Touch hole

One type of English gun cast in bronze

Loaded from muzzle. Powder shot ladled in. Barrel packed with wadding. Master gunner aims gun. Burning taper held to touch hole. Powder lit, gun fired.

First sighting of the Armada

▲ The Spanish fleet off the coast of Cornwall, July 29 1588

Legend has it that on the afternoon of Friday July 29, Drake was playing bowls on Plymouth Hoe. A captain sailing into Plymouth reported the first sighting of the Armada off Lizard Point, Cornwall.

▲ Drake playing bowls

When informed of the momentous news, Drake replied, 'We have time enough to finish the game and beat the Spaniards too!'

He certainly had time to finish his game as the tide was low. As the ebb tide freshened after 10pm, Howard, the royal galleons and the best-armed merchant ships were able to sail.

In the morning, Howard led 54 ships out at Eddystone to wait for the arrival of the Armada. As the Spanish fleet began its advance up the Channel and was sighted from land, lighted beacons sent the message through the country as far north as Durham.

On Sunday July 31, the Armada formed a battle order, and so each fleet, Spanish and English, was able to take stock of the other.

The English had kept their traditional line formation and were probably expecting the Spanish to do the same. They were, however, stunned at what they saw.

rmada attle ormation	Two easy 'prizes': Drake captures Rosario after a collision and San Salvador explodes and is captured	Portland Bill	English ships divided into four squadrons: Howard, Drake, Hawkins and Frobisher	Isle of Wight	Spanish move to Calais. No news from Parma.
nday July 31	Monday August 1	Tuesday August 2	Wednesday August 3	Thursday August 4	Friday August 5

The formidable crescent

What was it that the English saw?

The Spanish had manoeuvred themselves into a formidable defensive position rather like a crescent-shaped moon. The English had never seen anything like it before.

By adjusting the sails and varying the rate of the oarsmen's stroke, the Spanish had kept their ships tightly packed together. At the tips of the crescent were powerful warships. If the English tried to attack the weaker centre and the hulks, they could be surrounded and forced into hand-to-hand fighting on deck. This is what the Spanish wanted – and what the English wanted to avoid.

▲ The formidable crescent

The Spaniards, in turn, were taken aback by the speed and nimbleness of the English ships. Surprisingly, the Spanish did not attempt to land, as Sidonia was under strict orders from Philip to proceed up the Channel and join forces with Parma.

During the first week of the battle there were many skirmishes when Spanish and English ships were either cut off and rescued, or sailed out of trouble.

Yet by the time the Armada reached Calais not one English or Spanish ship had been sunk by enemy fire. Each battle had ended in stalemate.

Sidonia began to run out of ammunition. He kept sending messages to Parma to arrange a meeting but, puzzlingly, did not receive any replies.

On August 3 the English, to try to end the stalemate, decided to divide their ships into four squadrons. These proved more effective against straggling Spanish ships. By now, the English, too, were running out of gunpowder and cannon balls. Even with bigger guns of longer range and better trained gunners, they could not break that formidable defensive crescent.

Armada drops anchor at Calais	Sidonia requests 40 to 50 flyboats (little ships of war) from Parma	Parma builds about 12 flyboats at Dunkirk	Several built with rotten timbers and green planks	Parma had canal boats. These were for transporting cattle and had no masts, no sails, no guns.	Fireships launched

Saturday August 6   Sunday August 7

Hellburners

What tactics did the English adopt next?

They seized an opportunity when the Armada dropped anchor at Calais to wait for news from the Duke of Parma at Dunkirk.

After an urgent council of war, Howard and his captains decided to send in fireships to break up the formidable crescent. Eight old ships were immediately packed with inflammable materials – straw, gunpowder, tar, wood shavings and barrels of butter were all used. The ships were then coated with pitch. The plan was to set alight the ships and, helped by a favourable tide, a strong current and a fresh wind, launch them under cover of darkness. Guns aboard them had been specially primed so that when the heat was fierce enough, they would shoot at random among the Spanish ships.

Had the Spaniards anticipated this action?

Yes, indeed. Philip had warned Sidonia of the English and their terrible 'firework creations'.

In fact, the inventor of these 'hellburners', an Italian called Giambelli, was in England at the time. The mere mention of his name put fear into the hearts of the Spanish troops. Gossip said his 'bombs' could kill thousands. Unknown to the Spanish, however, Giambelli was actually engaged in London on quite another project altogether!

Sidonia organised a screen of pinnaces, armed with grappling irons and poles, to pull and push the burning ships away. At nearly midnight, lights were spotted at the edge of the English fleet. The hellburners had been launched.

I can see the Spanish galleons towering over the English ships.

▲ The launching of the fireships

Spanish ships re-form new crescent	Sidonia refuses to surrender	Hard wind forces Armada east-north-east. Skirmishes continue.	Threatened destruction of Spanish fleet on Zeeland sands. Wind changes.	Spanish retreat and are pursued north beyond Berwick-upon-Tweed for long journey home

| Monday August 8 | Last fight off Gravelines | Tuesday August 9 | | Friday August 12 |

'God blew and they were scattered'

The unmanned fireships bore down close together in line, sails set full and rigging alight. The screen of pinnaces moved forward within range of gunshot and snatched a pair of fireships, one either end, away from the line. The heat of the blaze made the guns fire at random, sending sprays of sparks into the pinnaces. These sheered off, the fireships broke through, and panic and confusion set in. Rather than stand off at sea, many ships ran with the wind after cutting anchor. The formidable crescent was broken at last!

Was that the end of the Armada?

No. Under the courageous leadership of Sidonia, the Spanish fleet re-grouped to renew the attack.

▲ Battle of Gravelines, August 8–10 1588

Then came the turning point of the conflict: the Battle of Gravelines on Monday, August 8.

By 4pm on this day the Spanish, despite much bravery, were struggling to survive. The only ammunition left was shot for muskets. There was so much slaughter that screams of death filled the air. Blood was seen dripping off the decks and priests knelt by dying men to comfort them. But captains refused to abandon ship. After a sudden storm, they re-formed again to fight, though many ships were badly damaged.

The wind forced them northwards. Another change of wind then rescued the fleet from certain destruction on the Zeeland sands. The English pursued them up the eastern coast to Berwick-upon-Tweed and left them, satisfied of victory.

Where was Parma?

The two ports where his barges were moored, Walcheren and Flushing, were held by the English and the Dutch. When at last he replied, he said he was helpless. Sidonia and Parma never did join forces.

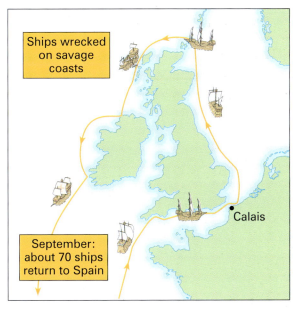

Ships wrecked on savage coasts

Calais

September: about 70 ships return to Spain

▲ The long journey home

God's own cause

Was that the end of a fear of invasion from the Spanish?

Though the Armada had been defeated, there was still a real fear that the Duke of Parma would attempt a landing from the Netherlands.

Elizabeth, despite concerns for her safety, decided to visit her troops. On August 18 she sailed down the River Thames in her royal barge to Tilbury.

Resplendent as ever in white and silver and riding a white horse, she inspected her adoring soldiers. She kept the number of her attendants deliberately small so every man could see her.

The following day, after a review and march past, she addressed her men. Her speech included these words:

'I know I have the body of a weak and feeble woman, but I have the heart and stomach of a king, and of a king of England too, and think foul scorn that Parma or Spain or any prince of Europe should dare invade the borders of my realm.'

But what did the victory achieve?

It proved that Elizabeth could govern in times of peace and war.

It pleased the Protestants of England, France, the Netherlands, Germany and Scandinavia, as they believed God was on their side. It showed the Catholics of France, Germany and Italy that Spain was beatable.

It had demonstrated on the Spanish side the extraordinary achievement of launching a huge fleet and on the English side that they could defend skilfully.

Perhaps the main legacy was the legend of the Armada itself. Both Elizabeth and the English people themselves began to think they were invincible against attack.

▲ 'The Armada Portrait', painted to celebrate England's victory. Elizabeth has one hand on the globe.

North-west: Discovered New Foundland (or 'Nova Scotia')	North-west: Hudson Bay and North American coastline	North-east: Attempted to find passage	North-east: Reached White Sea and Moscow and set up trading links	North-west: Reached Baffin Island	North-west: 3 voyages which failed to find passage to Spice Islands
1497/8 John Cabot	About 1509	1553 Sir Hugh Willoughby	1553/5 Richard Chancellor	1576 Martin Frobisher	1585–1587 John Davis

North-west, north-east

Why is Elizabeth's hand on the globe when it was Spain and Portugal which led the race for colonisation?

Since 1485 and the reign of Henry VII, England's place on the world map had changed dramatically.

The most famous voyage was that of Ferdinand Magellan, a Portuguese who circumnavigated the earth for the first time in 1519.

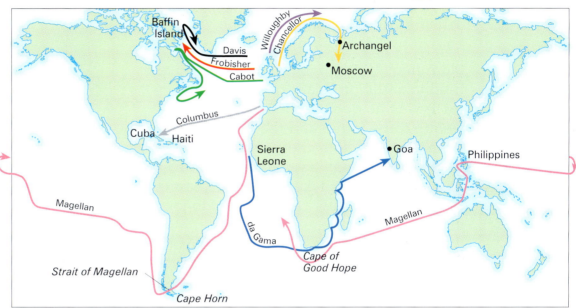

▲ A map to show the routes of the voyagers

By the middle of the 16th century, all the major trading centres in the world had been connected directly or indirectly by sea.

Because Portuguese and Spanish warships guarded their own trading routes, English sailors decided to seek a north-east or north-west passage to Asia.

In May 1553 Sir Hugh Willoughby and Richard Chancellor sailed north-east with three ships. Willoughby reached Russian Lapland, but he and his men froze to death.

Chancellor crossed the White Sea and reached the Russian port of Archangel. He then made a 1,500-mile journey by sledge to Moscow. On his return after meeting the Tsar, Ivan the Terrible, he set up the Muscovy (Russian) Company. He perished during a shipwreck on his next voyage.

Martin Frobisher and John Davis sailed north-west but could not find a passage to the Spice Islands.

In 1579 the Eastland Company took over the timber, tar and rope trades with the Baltic countries from the Hanseatic League. In the Mediterranean Sea, ships of the Turkey Company fought off pirates to reach the land of the Sultan. All these attempts at trading links were slowly helping to forge an empire.

| Smith wounded and captured by Indians when hunting | Chief Powhatten orders death by beating | 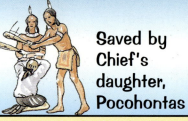 | Saved by Chief's daughter, Pocohontas | 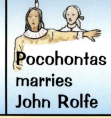 Pocohontas marries John Rolfe | Baptised as a Christian and comes to England | Unhappy with English climate | On her way home, she dies of smallpox at Gravesend |

1607 Pocohontas story   **1614**   **1617**

The first English colony

Elizabeth continued to encourage her sailors to establish trading routes. In 1584 she gave permission to one of her favourites, Sir Walter Raleigh, to colonise territory in North America. It was to be called Virginia, after a name she was known by – the Virgin Queen.

More than 100 colonists under Ralph Lane tried to settle on Roanoke Island, but there was no good harbour, no easy wealth to be found and the Indians there were hostile. The settlers returned home the following year. Soon afterwards, 15 new settlers were taken out to the same place. When further settlers went to join them the following year, all they discovered was a skeleton. They stayed for barely a month and then returned to England.

Raleigh financed in 1587 another attempt to found a colony in Virginia, but after two years none of the 150 settlers who landed there was found alive.

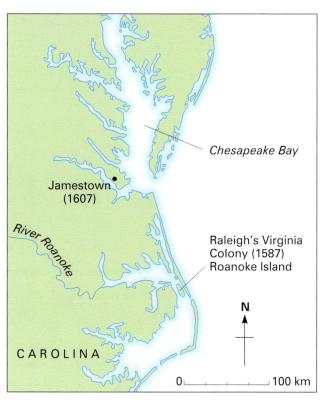

▲ Virginia, England's first colony

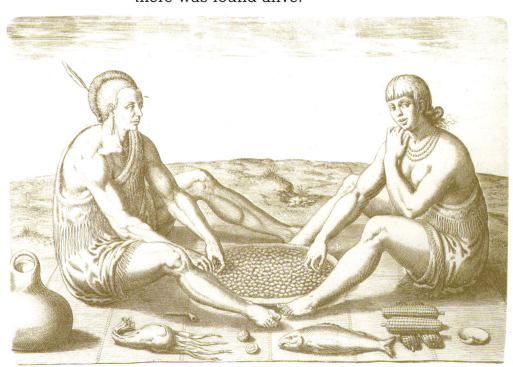

▲ Indians sharing a meal in about 1585

It was not until April 1607 that three ships landed in Chesapeake Bay in Virginia and founded Jamestown in honour of James I. Settlers struggled to survive. By September of that year, half the 104 colonists had died from typhoid or malaria and the 'Redskins' had become unfriendly. A soldier, John Smith, took over the leadership and saved the colony from mutiny, sickness and famine. Even by 1622, out of the 10,000 colonists who had sailed there, only 2,000 had survived.

One of the settlers, John Rolfe, founded the Virginian tobacco industry. With the labour of black slaves, this prospered.

48

India

Spain and Portugal were already well established in the East, and Englishmen had argued for some time about the best way to reach the wealth there.

On December 31 1600 Elizabeth I granted a charter to a group of merchants known as the East India Company. The charter's intention was to allow trade with the Middle and Far East, but the Dutch seized Portugal's possessions in Ceylon, Mauritius, South Africa and Indonesia.

The presence of Dutch warships in these parts forced the English to turn elsewhere, in particular to India.

India at this time was ruled by the Mogul Emperor Akbar. He controlled most of northern India and was the richest ruler on earth. A representative of the East India Company visited Akbar in 1601 to suggest trade with England, but Akbar died before arrangements could be made. It was not until 1610 that his son, the Emperor Jehangir, ignored Dutch and Portuguese pressure and reluctantly allowed the East India Company to have a trading 'factory' (base) at Surat.

In 1615 Sir Thomas Roe went as ambassador to the Mogul court. He advised the government back in England to increase trade by peaceful means. Much gold was sent to buy Indian indigo (a dye), spices and cotton goods. As control of the Mogul Empire grew weaker and India split into separate states, the English negotiated with individual princes to establish trading factories at Madras, Bombay and Calcutta. The foundation of a British empire in India had been laid.

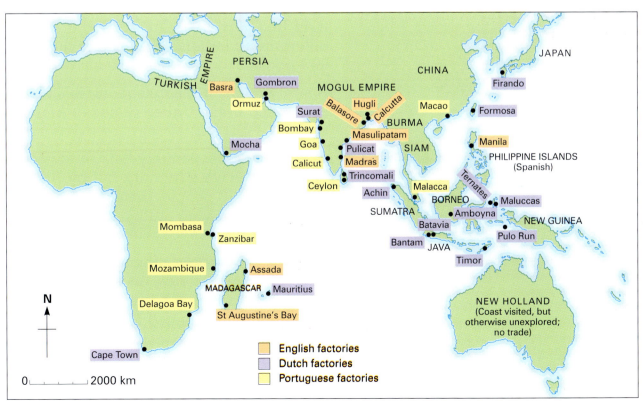

▲ A map to show the principal trading 'factories' in about 1650

The Mayflower leaves Southampton. 102 pilgrims amongst passengers.	20 acres Indian corn grown. Manured with dead herrings.	 English wheat failed, peas failed, barley 6 acres	Thanksgiving Day in United States of America: turkey, cranberry sauce, pumpkin pie
1620 September 6	**1621** Spring		Every November

More colonists leave England

Some settlers sailed to colonies for religious reasons. In England you could be fined and punished if you did not follow the services of the Church of England. One group of people, the Separatist Puritans, decided to sail to Virginia where they could practise their religious beliefs in freedom.

On September 6 1620 these 'pilgrims' set off in a small sailing ship called the *Mayflower*. Supplies were inadequate and storms blew the ship off course. However, after landing on Cape Cod in November, they founded a settlement, New Plymouth, on December 11 1620.

▲ The *Mayflower* sails from Southampton

Before their arrival, they had organised their government by the terms of the Mayflower Compact. The heads of 41 families on board agreed to choose their own governor and re-elect him if they wished.

Sadly, during the first winter, 51 of the colonists died of scurvy and illness. Despite this, they persisted and slowly established their settlement.

Helped by an Indian, Squanto, they planted corn. Twenty acres were grown, and the remaining pilgrims celebrated their first harvest, thanking God and entertaining Indians to a feast of turkey and goose.

A similar feast of Thanksgiving is still celebrated in the United States of America today.

Life was still desperately hard, and not all Indian tribes were friendly, but by 1624 more than 120 people, including new settlers, were living at Plymouth, New England.

Success encouraged others to settle in the New World of America, and in 1691 the Plymouth plantation became part of a larger settlement called Massachusetts. New England thus became a thriving English Colony.

nitarians: eny trinity nd divinity f Christ	Quakers: no ministers, no set services, silent worship	Baptists: adult baptism	Independents: worship of English Church considered idolatry	Separatists (Congregationalists): those who stay away from churches and worship in private meetings	All known as Dissenters and later Nonconformists

ome different forms of Puritanism

Puritans

Who were the Separatist Puritans?

The word 'Puritan' comes from the word 'purify' (to cleanse).

Separatists and other groups of Puritans wanted to purify the Church of England of anything to do with the Catholic way of worshipping. They wanted to get rid of priests, bishops, the prayer book, altars, candles – anything that came between a person and his God, as they saw it.

All Puritan groups were united against the Church of England because they felt it allowed both good and wicked people in its congregations of worshippers.

They thought themselves to be God's elected ones, or 'saints'. As saints, they believed they had been specially chosen by God to live in close fellowship with their own people.

▲ A Puritan family in Elizabethan times

Each congregation chose its own minister. He preached from the Bible and led a plain form of worship. Some groups such as the Separatists did not worship in a church, but held their own private meetings.

Family life was important to the Puritans. The father led the family and servants in prayer, gave religious instruction and taught his children to read the Bible. Sunday, the Sabbath, was given over entirely to God. Families prayed, worshipped, listened to sermons and read from the scriptures. There was no time to be idle in a Puritan household, no swearing and no dishonesty. Pastimes such as football, theatre and dancing were regarded as frivolous, and even music in church was frowned upon. As businessmen, Puritans were respected. They charged fair prices and there was no cheating or money-lending.

The actual number of Puritans was never large but their influence in Parliament was to prove enormous.

▲ A Puritan family in Stuart times

① Act of Supremacy: monarch became Supreme Governor of the Church of England

② Act of Uniformity: brought back English Book of Common Prayer

③ Set of Injunctions

④ 39 Articles clergymen had to agree to

1559 The four laws of the Elizabethan settlement

1560

Elizabethan settlement

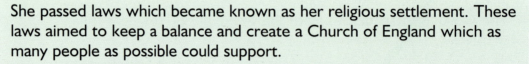

If Elizabeth was Protestant, how did she deal with the Puritans and Catholics?

She passed laws which became known as her religious settlement. These laws aimed to keep a balance and create a Church of England which as many people as possible could support.

Above all, Elizabeth wanted a united country, but she was well aware that many people still believed in the Catholic faith which had been established for over a thousand years.

Supreme Governor of Church of England

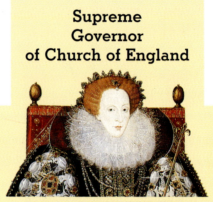

Puritans influenced by Calvin; Presbyterians; Nonconformists; Dissenters

Catholics

Anglican Protestants influenced by Luther, but kept some Catholic traditions

Loyal to Crown

Wanted to get rid of last signs of Catholicism

Wanted no special garments for parson

Wanted more emphasis on sermons

Wanted rid of wedding rings

Wanted no sign of cross to be made over child's head at baptism

Wanted kneeling in church to be left to discretion of minister

Furious when Elizabeth excommunicated by Pope

Presbyterian Puritans did not want bishops

People still worshipped at altars

Parsons still wore vestments of priests

Parsons could get married

Everyone to go to church on Sundays

Bible readings and church services in English

Words of Communion service carefully written

Believed bread and wine were symbols of Christ

Many Catholics loyal to Crown

Many practised religion in private and were tolerated

In 1570 the Pope excommunicated Elizabeth and said English and Welsh Catholics need not obey her as Queen

In 1571 special law passed stating it was illegal to support any other claims to the throne: punishment was death for High Treason

It became dangerous to be a practising Catholic

Catholics suspected of plots against the Queen: some of these involved Mary Queen of Scots

orthern ebellion. Mary nvolved. 00 hanged.	Ridolfi plot. Mary involved. Norfolk executed.	Throckmorton plot. Mary involved. Throckmorton executed.	Parry's plot	Babington plot. Mary involved. Babington executed.	Execution of Mary Queen of Scots	Various plots: Polwhele, Yorke, Williams, Lopez, Squire	Rebellion. Earl of Essex executed.
569	1571	1583	1585	1586	1587 February 8	1590s	1601

THE STUARTS
10

Mary Queen of Scots

Elizabeth was never free of plots against her. Such plots all demonstrated the struggle for power between Protestants and Catholics. At the centre of four of these plots was Elizabeth's cousin, Mary, a Catholic.

Mary had been Queen of Scotland since 1542 when a week old and Queen of France since 1559 through marriage to Francis II. But, after his death in 1560, she returned to Scotland.

There she married her Catholic cousin, Lord Darnley. Shortly after the birth of their son, James, Darnley was murdered. Mary then married the Earl of Bothwell, who was soon accused, and then acquitted, of Darnley's murder.

The Protestant nobles rose against Mary, who was forced to give up the throne in favour of her son who, in a Protestant church, was crowned James VI of Scotland.

Mary fled to England where she was held captive by Elizabeth for 21 years, although she was treated very well. During this time, she was involved in various plots to overthrow Elizabeth, and it was the Babington plot of 1586 which marked her downfall.

Babington worked from Paris to release Mary but his group was infiltrated by government spies posing as Catholics. A brewer, who concealed letters between Mary and Babington, was bribed. The letters were intercepted, codes were deciphered, possible forged postscripts added and the letters copied.

Written evidence of a plan to assassinate Elizabeth condemned Babington and Mary. Babington confessed and was hanged. Mary herself was found guilty of High Treason. This led to her being beheaded on February 8th, 1587, after Elizabeth reluctantly signed a death warrant.

▲ Mary Queen of Scots – a nineteenth-century engraving based on a portrait painted when Mary was alive

▲ The execution of Mary Queen of Scots

Death of Elizabeth I. No direct heir.	James VI of Scotland becomes James I of England			Chosen design flown from 'jack staff' on ship's bowsprit	

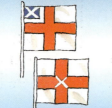

1603	Possible designs to combine Scottish and English flags	1606 First Union Flag

James I, the first Stuart

Did Catholic plots end with the death of Elizabeth I?

Not at all. When James VI of Scotland, son of Mary Queen of Scots, succeeded as James I of England in 1603, he too had to deal with Catholic conspiracies.

▲ James I of England/James VI of Scotland

Though a Protestant, he was prepared to be tolerant towards Catholics as long as they were loyal to the Crown. Any act of disloyalty towards him was seen by James to be an act of disloyalty towards God.

Why was this?

Because James believed in the 'Divine Right' to rule his subjects.

He knew beyond all doubt whatsoever that this power of Divine Right had been given to him by God. So sure was he of this absolute power that one pamphlet – and he wrote many – was called *The Mystical Reverence that belongs to Him that sits on the Throne of God*.

However, his tolerance towards Catholics did not last. When he stopped enforcing laws against celebrating Mass, Catholics gathered together openly again. As this displeased the Protestants, James, in 1604, commanded that all priests, including Jesuits, should leave England.

Jesuits were a militant order of Catholic priests, founded by a Spaniard. They encouraged the destruction of Protestantism. They had conspired with Mary and since the Armada they had plotted against Elizabeth. They were certainly not prepared to be loyal to James.

The Jesuits and the more extreme Catholics were hoping for Spanish support to overthrow James. When this was not forthcoming, another plot was hatched.

▲ Jesuit priests

Catesby reveals plot to Thomas Winter and John Wright	Fawkes returns after 12 years abroad	Main conspirators meet and take oath	Percy obtains sub-tenancy of building next to Parliament House	Digging and abandoning of tunnel	Percy rents vault	Gunpowder stored ready
1604 Lent	April	May 20	May 24	December–January	1605 May	May

The Gunpowder plot

What was the actual plot?

A group of Catholics planned to destroy the Protestant government by leading a rebellion, to place one of the royal children as more or less a puppet on the throne, and take over the government themselves.

The idea was to blow up the House of Lords at the State Opening of Parliament in 1605. The explosion would kill the King and Queen, some of their children, other members of the royal family, peers, judges, lawyers and members of the House of Commons.

The leader of the conspirators, Robert Catesby, was already known to the government for his involvement in the Essex rebellion and his connection with the Jesuits.

The other chief conspirators were, like Catesby, Catholic gentry: gentlemen from established families. Some of these, too, were known to the government.

John Wright
Good swordsman. Loyal to Catesby. In plot from beginning. Active in Essex rebellion.

Thomas Percy
Cousin of Duke of Northumberland. Position at court as Captain-of-the-Pensioners-in-Ordinary. In plot from beginning.

Robert Winter
Winter brothers related by blood or marriage to all the chief plotters except Guido (Guy) Fawkes. Robert advised caution.

Robert Catesby
Born leader: handsome and brave but a liar and a gambler. Became fanatical Catholic after the deaths of father and wife. Able to persuade others to follow him, even die for him. Involved in Essex rebellion.

Christopher Wright
Younger brother of John.

Guido Fawkes
Close friend of the Wright brothers. Brave soldier who had been out of country for 12 years. Fanatical Catholic.

Bates
Servant. Drawn into plot later.

Thomas Winter
Younger brother of Robert. A captain in the army. Good linguist and diplomat. In plot from beginning.

▲ An engraving of the conspirators, made more than 100 years after the plot

Scheming and secrecy

How did they manage to get close to the House of Lords?

Percy, because of his position at Court, was able to rent a building, Prince's Chamber, next to Parliament House.

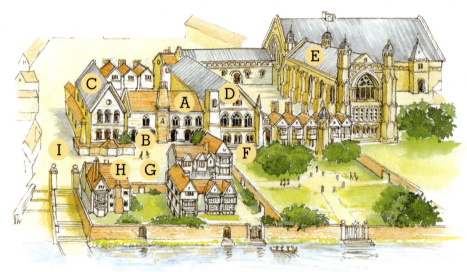

In December 1604 seven of the conspirators began to dig a tunnel from Prince's Chamber to the House of Lords, but, by the end of January, it had filled with water and the plan was abandoned.

Luckily for the plotters, a ground-floor storage-room under the Painted Chamber suddenly became available. Percy rented this and 36 barrels of gunpowder were smuggled in by river and stored there.

▲ The Houses of Parliament at the time of James I

Key

A The House of Lords

B Chamber under the House of Lords

C The Prince's Chamber

D The Painted Chamber

E The House of Commons

F Vault under the Painted Chamber

G Yard into which door from **B** opened

H Passage from **G** leading to Parliament Place

I Parliament Place

Where did they get the gunpowder from?

It was readily available from merchants. Ships, the Militia (non-professional army) and the Trained Bands of London (better-drilled men) all used it. Some was even used on the stage in the theatres in London.

As Parliament was postponed until October 1605, Catesby left for the Midlands where Catholic friends lived and where Jesuit priests were active.

He needed to organise forces to help the rebellion. He needed rich Catholics with funds, and safe houses to hoard arms, ammunition and keep horses. New supporters joined and, though some had grave misgivings, Catesby convinced them that the enterprise had been approved by the Catholic Church. Parliament was postponed again until November 5.

arker in ssex bellion	Changes to Protestant religion	Catholic friends include conspirators	Parker made Lord Monteagle. In his service was Thomas Winter.	Salisbury head of secret service	Monteagle's name erased or pasted over in documents examining conspirators	Praised by Salisbury at trial for discretion and fidelity	£700 a year for delivering letter
602	1603			1604			

Bomb scare

Towards the end of October, a Lord Monteagle ordered his servants to open up one of his rarely used London homes. On October 26 he dined there, attended only by his gentlemen and pages. At about 7 o'clock one of his pages brought him a letter which had been handed to him outside in the dark by a stranger. The letter had neither date nor signature.

'My lord . . . out of the love I bear to some of your friends, I have a care of your preservation. Therefore I warn you . . . to devise some excuse to shift your attendance at this Parliament . . . they shall receive a terrible blow this Parliament and yet they shall not see who hurts them . . . The danger is past as soon as you have burnt this letter.'

Monteagle took the letter to the Earl of Salisbury, who showed it to the King.

▲ The letter which Lord Monteagle received

What did the King decide to do?

The King immediately thought of gunpowder, as his father, Lord Darnley, had been murdered in a gunpowder plot in 1567.

He ordered a search of Parliament House. During the first search, a man found guarding fuel in a cellar said he was a servant of Thomas Percy. During a second search at just after midnight the same man was arrested in possession of a watch, slow matches, touchwood and a lantern.

In the presence of the King, he gave his name as John Johnson.

In the Tower of London, under questioning and torture, he gave his real name, Guido Fawkes, on November 7. On November 8, after further torture (this time on the rack), and having given his accomplices time to escape, he named them.

▲ The Eye of God on Fawkes

Please to remember,
The fifth of November,
Gunpowder treason and plot.

I see no reason,
Why gunpowder treason,
Should ever be forgot.

Penny for the guy

Cellars searched every year on eve of State Opening of Parliament

1605   1678

Treason

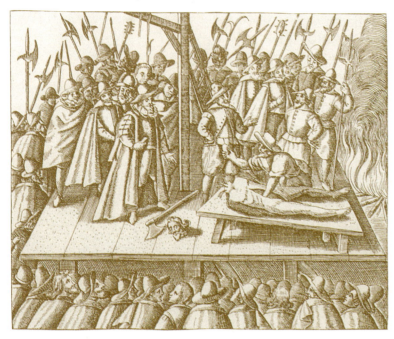

▲ A public death for the conspirators

Did Catesby and the others escape?

Amazingly, they continued with their plans to recruit further supporters, only to find that many were deserting them.

A remaining band of about 60 fugitives took refuge at Holbeach House, near Stourbridge, Staffordshire. There, surrounded by forces of two local sheriffs, they either surrendered, were wounded or were killed. Catesby and Percy, standing back to back, were killed by two bullets from one musket shot.

Surviving conspirators were tried for High Treason and sentenced to death by hanging, disembowelling and quartering. Fawkes, weak from torture, could barely climb the ladder. Near the top he leapt, breaking his neck in the fall.

Three Jesuit priests were implicated in the plot. One, Father Garnet, Superior of Jesuits in England, was captured, tried for High Treason and hanged. By dragging the condemned through the streets on hurdles, the government was able publicly to discredit English Catholics. Subsequently, under a new Act, all Catholics were required to take an oath of supremacy, agreeing that the Pope could not depose kings.

Were government spies involved in the Gunpowder plot too?

Evidence suggests they were.

Certainly, coincidences were convenient: the suddenly available vault, the mysterious letter arriving at a rarely used house, November 5 being a 'lucky day' for James I, as on the same day in 1600 he had been saved from another plot.

Key people such as Phelippes, a forgerer and decipherer, and Sir William Waad, the chief prosecutor, were involved in the Babington plot too.

Plots involve lies, scheming and secrecy. Finding the truth about them is difficult, but it makes the study of history fascinating.

Gwido fawkes

Guido

▲ Guido Fawkes's autographs before and after torture

58

arlier ranslations f the Bible	William Tyndale	Miles Coverdale	Bible in English to be placed in every parish church	The Great Bible (Matthew)	Reading of Bible limited to clerics, noblemen, gentry and merchants	The Bishop's Bible	The Authorised Version of the Bible (King James)
	1525–1531	1535–1537	1538 August	1539	1543	1569	1611

The King James Bible

How did James deal with the Puritans?

James respected them as they were loyal to the Crown, and at the Hampton Court Conference in 1604 he and his bishops considered a petition from them.

They made various requests and James agreed to some, such as appointing more ministers to preach sermons, but he remained firm on keeping all the ceremonies as they were in Elizabeth's time.

Ministers had to wear their surplices in church, use a ring in marriage services, make the sign of the cross in baptism and so forth. As a determined Protestant, James enforced the findings of the Hampton Court Conference.

James was personally very knowledgeable about theology (the study of religion) and it was his interest and support that led to the publication of a new Bible written in English.

Why did James want that?

Because clergy and people had, up to this time, read and listened to various translations and editions of the Bible.

James approved of one version written in clear straightforward English that everyone could understand. Very fairly he chose respected Puritan scholars among his selection of 54 translators, the 'best learned' from the universities of Oxford and Cambridge. Work began in 1604 and the new Authorised Version of the Bible was published in 1611. Every church was ordered to use it, and by the end of the 17th century there were perhaps as many as half a million printed bibles in England.

It became known throughout the whole of the English-speaking world and remained unchanged for over 300 years, a lasting tribute to James and his scholars.

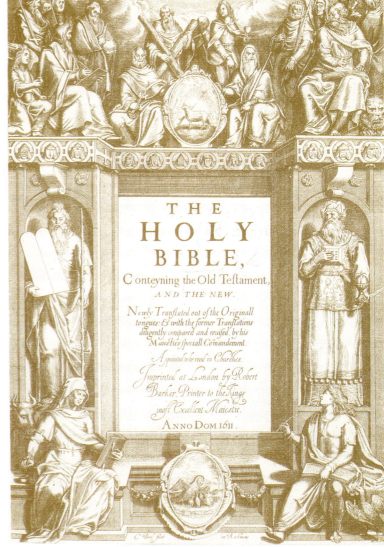

▲ The title page of the King James Bible

59

Union of the crowns of England, Scotland, Ireland	Union of the kingdoms difficult as no one law, religion, or political system	'Old English' lords: descendants of Norman-English barons. 'New English' Protestant settlers.	No Tudor or Stuart monarch ever visited Ireland	Joined to England by Acts of Union 1536 and 1543

1603	Ireland	Wales

Ireland and Wales

Was James I King of Ireland and Wales as well as King of Scotland and England?

He was King of Ireland because Henry VIII had taken that title in 1541 after the Reformation when England became Protestant.

Lord Deputies in Ireland hoped to make the Irish follow English law and speak English rather than follow Gaelic laws and language. They did manage to control the south and organise Ireland into counties, but the northern part of Ulster remained Gaelic.

In 1595 the Earl of Tyrone became leader of Gaelic Ireland, but was defeated in 1603. This meant England had conquered the whole of Ireland. James I's government decided to carry on with the Tudor idea of 'plantation'.

What did 'plantation' mean?

It meant settlement by colonists.

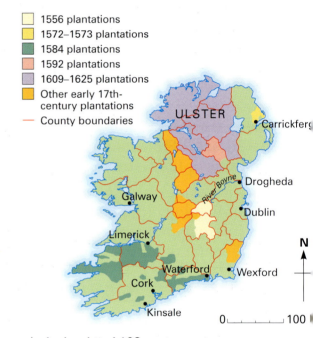

- 1556 plantations
- 1572–1573 plantations
- 1584 plantations
- 1592 plantations
- 1609–1625 plantations
- Other early 17th-century plantations
- County boundaries

▲ Ireland in 1603

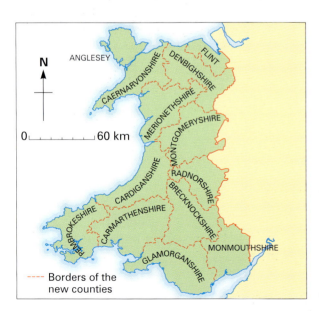

▲ Wales in 1536, after the first Act of Union

The English thought that the Irish were dangerous because they were Catholic, Gaelic and uncivilised. By 'planting' Protestant settlers in Ulster, many of them Presbyterian Scots, they hoped that Protestant beliefs and ways of life would 'improve' the Irish. The 'New English' settlers tended to regard themselves as conquerors of the 'Old English'.

James was not King of Wales because, through two Acts of Union in 1536 and 1543, Wales had been joined with England. In 1536 Marcher lordships had been divided into shires. English law and county administration extended into Wales. The Welsh were allowed to continue speaking their own language and elect 24 Members of Parliament.

In 1543 the whole of Wales was put under the supervision of the Council of Wales. Travelling law courts called 'Great Sessions' carried out the same job as Courts of Assize in England.

onnage and oundage customs: uties on imports nd exports	Selling crown land and titles	Reviving old feudal taxes	Raising forced loans from merchants	Granting monopolies – the sole rights to manufacture, sell or import goods, e.g. starch, currants, glass

aising money in Tudor and Stuart times

English Parliament

Did Scotland and England share the same Parliament in the early 1600s?

No, only the same king.

In Scotland, James governed with the help of a Parliament called the Three Estates – lords, bishops and representatives of the people who sat in one place. In England, James had to get used to a different system.

The English Parliament had three parts: the king, the House of Lords and the House of Commons.

The House of Lords was made up of the nobility and bishops.

The House of Commons was made up of knights of the shires, representatives of the Welsh shires, burgesses representing boroughs, merchants and lawyers.

Members of both houses were wealthy men of property.

It was against tradition for monarchs to enter the House of Commons. Privy Councillors kept them informed of proceedings.

Parliament had two main functions:

- To make laws. Laws started as Bills in the House of Commons. They then had to be passed by the Lords and the king before they became full Acts of Parliament (known as Statutes). The king could veto (overrule) Bills.

- To provide the king with extra ways of taxation in times of emergency, such as war. The Commons voted for these taxes (known as subsidies).

As James's finances grew weaker, the influence of the Commons grew stronger.

Why did his finances grow weaker?

▲ James I in the House of Lords. His son, later Charles I, sits at his side.

▲ The House of Commons at around the time of Charles I

James thought he had taken over a rich country and spent money lavishly. He and his son, Charles, needed money for wars. They also needed money for their Court favourites, particularly George Villiers, the Duke of Buckingham.

Master of the Horse	Knight of the Garter	Baron, then Viscount	Earl Privy Councillor	Master of the Wardrobe	Marquis, then Lord High Admiral	Duke of Buckingham	Coach wrecked by angry sailors	Mutiny in front of his house	His astrologer is hacked to pieces	Murdered by deranged lieutenant
George Villiers		1617				1623	1626	1628 March	June	August 23

Charles I

▲ The Villiers family, 1628

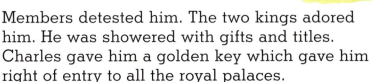

Did Parliament resent Buckingham?

Members detested him. The two kings adored him. He was showered with gifts and titles. Charles gave him a golden key which gave him right of entry to all the royal palaces.

This picture shows how favoured he was. The Duke and Duchess (holding hands) are surrounded by two earls (one held by his nurse), two countesses, a viscount and a future duchess!

His influence on James and Charles led to England being involved in disastrous wars against Spain in 1624 and France in 1626. Buckingham led costly and unnecessary military expeditions, all of which ended in failure.

Parliament tried to get rid of him. At Charles's first Parliament in 1625, when Buckingham was mentioned by name as being incompetent, the King, to protect him, dissolved Parliament.

At the second Parliament in 1626, the Commons tried to impeach Buckingham. Charles again dissolved Parliament.

What is impeachment?

It is a political trial when the Commons act as prosecutors and the Lords act as judges and jury.

At the third Parliament of 1628, Charles was presented with a Petition of Rights. Both houses wanted certain grievances, such as imprisonment without trial, put right.

Charles signed, but the campaign against Buckingham continued. In August 1628 Buckingham was murdered by an unpaid army officer.

Charles was grief-stricken. Parliament and Londoners, however, were delighted.

In 1629 there were extraordinary scenes in the Commons. The Speaker (chairman) was held down in his chair while resolutions over taxation and religion running against the King's wishes were pushed through. Charles dissolved Parliament, determined now to rule without it.

▲ Charles I

nglish folk had   monopoly butter   monopoly pins   monopoly hay
o buy: monopoly herrings   monopoly buttons   monopoly coaches
onopoly bricks   monopoly wine   monopoly belts   monopoly dice
onopoly coal   monopoly salt   monopoly glass
onopoly currants   monopoly tobacco   monopoly starch   monopoly mousetraps

onopolies

The King's personal rule

How did Charles raise taxes without Parliament?

He used various ways and means.

He used his prerogative (royal authority) to continue collecting Tonnage and Poundage, even though the Commons had been increasingly reluctant to grant it.

He also used his prerogative to extend another tax, Ship Money.

This had previously been collected from coastal towns and ports for the upkeep of the navy: a strong fleet was essential to protect English shores from pirates and even slave-raiders.

When inland towns and counties were ordered to pay Ship Money from 1635, a Puritan landowner and Member of Parliament, John Hampden, refused. He declared the tax illegal. He lost his case by seven votes to five, but received countrywide publicity. One of his many supporters in Parliament was his cousin, Oliver Cromwell.

Cromwell was one landowner who chose to pay a refusal fine rather than to observe an ancient feudal law that Charles decided to revive: owners of land worth £40 or more had to become knights or pay.

The granting of monopolies, which had always been unpopular, was also revived by Charles.

▲ This glorious ship, *Sovereign of the Seas*, was built with Ship Money. The engraving was to demonstrate that Charles was right to charge the tax.

Why were they unpopular?

Because unfavoured tradesmen lost their jobs and prices rose.

In 1633 a new monopoly soap company, used by Catholics, made inferior 'popish' soap which burnt the skin. It was rumoured that its use would corrupt the body and perhaps the soul.

Discontent over taxes and 'popish practices' simmered away during these 11 years – discontent which was ready to come to the boil.

63

Believed in free will – to act and decide own fate	Worship was centred on the altar rather than the pulpit	Authority of clergy, especially bishops, strengthened	Valued order and holiness in services	Rejected hatred of popery

Arminians

William Laud

Were there other 'popish' practices?

Parliament thought so. Although Charles was the first king to be brought up in the Church of England and felt it his duty before God to preserve it, Parliament felt he favoured Catholics.

▲ Queen Henrietta Maria

It was noted that his wife, the French princess Henrietta Maria, was Catholic. She had a large following at Court and took courtiers and the royal children openly to mass.

Parliament also distrusted the Archbishop of Canterbury, William Laud.

He and Charles supported the Dutch theologian, Arminius. Arminians promoted well-ordered churches and rich ceremonies – all the practices Charles I liked and which Puritans thought were 'popish'. With the King's backing, Laud reorganised the Church of England. He saw much to improve. It was quite common then to see churches with broken doors and windows. Laud found communion tables being used as hat-stands and foot-rests. Even dogs found tables convenient. Laud insisted on changes. Tables had to be moved to the east-end of the chancel. They were to be railed off from disrespectful parishioners and dogs. Priests had to wear correct robes and to bow to the altar.

Critics of the Church were severely punished. One famous case involved three Puritans, William Prynne, Henry Burton and John Bastwicke. All three were convicted of criticising Church policies and sentenced to heavy fines, solitary confinement for life and the loss of their ears.

On their day of punishment, sympathetic and angry Londoners lay down sweet herbs in their path and gave them cups of wine.

Gestures such as these indicated Laud's unpopularity in England. When changes were attempted in the Scottish Kirk, however, gestures were far more dramatic.

▲ Laud eats ears for supper

cots ordered to eplace Knox's Book f Common Order rith the Book of ommon Prayer	Prayer-book contained 'popish' images such as angels	Covenanters' banners	Pacification of Berwick	Scots invasion	Treaty of Ripon – high indemnity and daily allowance to be paid to Scots
637 July		1639	June	1640	October

The Scottish Kirk

I thought Scotland had a different Church?

It did: the Presbyterian Kirk based on Calvinist principles.

The Kirk was controlled by committees of clergy, nobles and gentry. Charles and Laud wanted to bring the Kirk in line with the Church of England.

In July 1637, without consulting the committees, the King ordered the Church of England prayer book to be used throughout Scotland. The Scots thought it 'popish' and many ministers refused to use it. Those who did use it sparked riots. Uproar spread and ministers and nobility organised resistance.

A document of 1580, which claimed to be the founding charter of the Kirk, was revived. Crowds flocked to sign it and it became known as the Covenant.

▲ Riots in the Kirk

Charles decided to crush the Covenanters' rebellion. But in 1639 his untrained and badly-equipped army soon mutinied and fled from the well-organised Covenanters. Charles was forced to negotiate peace terms.

While the Scottish Parliament discussed peace, Charles was advised by his Chief Minister, Strafford, to call Parliament to discuss war. The leader of the Commons, John Pym, refused to grant war tax unless grievances over taxation and religion were met.

Charles dissolved this short Parliament of three weeks in May 1640.

Strafford tried to raise a forced loan to pay for the war. Four aldermen who refused to pay were thrown into prison. Strafford had also raised an army of mainly Irish Catholics to fight the war. However, before he could bring them over, the Scots invaded England, took Newcastle-upon-Tyne and demanded occupation costs. A bankrupt Charles had to call a Parliament to pay the Scots to leave England.

Thomas Wentworth helps write Petition of Rights in Commons	Moves to King's service	Nicknamed 'Black Tom the Tyrant'	President of Council of the North	Lord Deputy of Ireland	Created Earl of Strafford, Knight of the Garter	Impeachment for High Treason	Army plot	Bill of Attainder	Execution
1629					1640 January	1641 March	March–May	April	May 12

Strafford

Immediately Parliament was called in November 1640, Pym united the two Houses against the King's ministers, Strafford and Laud. Both were impeached and sent to the Tower of London. There Laud remained until his execution in 1645. Strafford was brought to trial at Westminster Hall in March 1641.

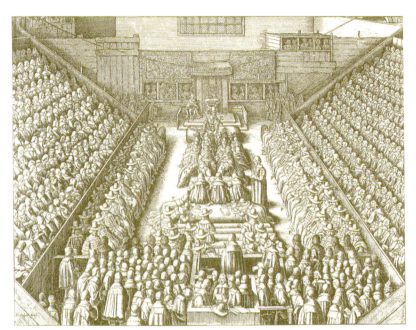

On what charge?

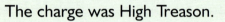

The charge was High Treason.

Among the 28 charges, it was alleged that Strafford had intended using the Irish army against the King's peaceful subjects. Strafford defended himself brilliantly and, as there was only one unsupported witness, the impeachment failed.

The Commons then used an ancient custom, called a Bill of Attainder, against Strafford. This declared his guilt without the need for a formal trial – and without proof.

Surely the King vetoed this Bill?

The King promised the Lords that he would veto it, and he promised Strafford he would save his life. But at this time there were wild rumours of an army plot involving English Catholics who would release Strafford and dissolve Parliament. Fear and distrust of Catholics led to shops closing and rioting in the streets. Angry citizens threatened the lives of lords who had voted against the Bill of Attainder. On May 8, the Lords passed the Bill.

On May 9 mobs surrounded Whitehall. Strafford, putting his country first, wrote to the King urging him to sign the Bill. Charles, fearing for the safety of his Queen, his family and his kingdom, decided to sacrifice his minister and signed the Bill.

▲ The trial and execution of the Earl of Strafford

Three days later, Strafford was executed. Charles never forgave himself for breaking his word to Strafford. He had lost a courageous and most able minister. Parliament still had Pym.

rom Spanish word 'caballeros', eaning 'trooper on horse back'. arliamentarians used it as term f abuse against Royalists.

CAVALIERS v. ROUNDHEADS
Royalists   Parliamentarians

Nickname of London apprentices who cut hair short to create a bullet-headed look. Royalists used it as term of abuse against Parliamentarians.

'King' Pym

Why didn't Charles dissolve the 1640 Parliament and so prevent these things happening?

Because during the panic over the army plot, Pym rushed through a Bill which prevented the King from dissolving it.

When Charles signed this, Pym went on to weaken the King's power to govern even more. In January 1641 all taxes introduced without Parliament's authority – including Ship Money and Customs – were declared illegal, the prerogative courts were abolished, and the King was required to call Parliament every third year.

The Irish rose up against the fear of possible Puritan rule. Several thousand Protestants in Ireland were murdered. The King asked Parliament for money to pay for an army to restore order in Ireland. However, Pym thought the King might use the money against his enemies in Parliament. He therefore demanded that Parliament should have control of the army. He also prepared a Grand Remonstrance.

What was that?

A document condemning all Charles's policies and suggesting reform.

Mafter PYM
HIS SPEECH
In *Parliament*, on *Wednefday*, the fifth of *January*, 1641.
Concerning the Vote of the Houfe of Commons, for his difcharge upon the Accufation of High Treafon, exhibited againft himfelfe, and the Lord *Kimbolton*, Mr. *Iohn Hampden*, Sr. *Arthur Haſſerig*, Mr. *Strowd*, M. *Hollis*, by his Maiefty,

The true Effigies of Mr *Iohn Pym*, Efquire

London Printed for I.W, 1641.

▲ The cover of a copy of Pym's speech attacking Charles for taxing the country without Parliament's consent

▲ A Cavalier with feathers, ribbon and lace

It was presented in Parliament by Oliver Cromwell, but was passed by only 11 votes. A Royalist group, thinking 'King' Pym had gone too far, rallied round Charles.

Pym, in turn, stirred up mobs of apprentices (Roundheads) who broke into Westminster Hall and were chased out at sword-point by the King's officers (Cavaliers).

Over Christmas the mood in London became violent. Armed bands roamed the streets and mobs ran wild. In January 1642 rumours reached the King that Pym had threatened to impeach Queen Henrietta Maria herself. Charles decided to act.

The road to war

What did Charles do?

He ordered the impeachment of Pym and four other powerful Members of Parliament.

▲ Charles enters the House of Commons

Accompanied by an armed following of 400 cavalry, the King went to the Commons himself to arrest them. As he entered, the House fell into an utter, tense silence. He asked for each of the five men by name, but the Speaker refused to say if they were present. Charles then saw the empty seats.

'I see the birds have flown,' he remarked.

Pym and the others, informed by spies, had escaped two hours earlier by barge down the River Thames. The King's attempt to grasp supreme power had failed.

In entering Parliament by force rather than by invitation, he was seen as trying to destroy its liberties and privileges. This action lost him the support of his capital city. Women boiled water to pour over the heads of Royalist soldiers. Catholic houses were attacked and several Catholic priests were murdered. Crowds filled the streets as open rebellion broke out. The trained bands defended Parliament against the King. Barricades were set up and cannon moved into firing positions.

London was no longer safe for Charles. He left on January 10 1642, never to return as an acknowledged king. On January 11 Pym and his friends returned in triumph by river to Westminster.

Cromwell suggested that a committee be set up 'to consider the means to put the kingdom in a posture of defence'. Both king and Parliament then drew up plans for defence.

On August 22 1642 Charles raised his standard in a field near Nottingham. Civil War had begun.

35 different battles	Killed in battle: Parliament 34,000 Royalist 51,000	Taken prisoner: Parliament 34,000 Royalist 83,000	Died from disease: 100,000 Many more soldiers crippled for life

Civil War estimates

Friend or foe?

The Civil War was a terrible event in English history.

Why was it so terrible?

Civil wars, when people of the same nation take up arms against each other, are the worst kinds of war. For many people, the English Civil War was a war of conscience. Men and women had to decide whether to put loyalty to the Royalist or Parliamentarian cause before loyalty to friends and families.

Not only would villages fight villages and neighbours fight neighbours, but fathers might oppose sons or sons-in-law and brothers would face brothers. A woman could be married to a Royalist but be sister to a Parliamentarian, and so forth.

Casualties, too, in comparison with other wars, were greater. More than half of the pitched battles ever fought on English soil were fought during this war.

Who joined which side?

Most, but not all, of the House of Lords joined the Royalists. Those who disliked changes in religion, politics or society in general sided with the King. Those who disliked Laud and Arminianism tended to join the Parliamentarians. Many wanted no part in it. Others joined whichever side arrived in their area first and forced them to join.

Parliamentarian forces controlled the wealthier south and east, and all the ports except Newcastle-upon-Tyne. The navy sided with Parliament. The King needed to win quickly.

Soldiers of both armies

A pike was part club, part spear

The butt-end of a gun was used as a club; re-loading was slow

▲ Pikeman (infantry)

▲ Cavalry

▲ Musketeer (infantry)

Only in Heaven

Pro Deo et Patria
'For God and Country'

For ỹ Caufe of ỹ Lord
I draw my Sword

Sir Thomas Fairfax, the Earl of Essex, the Earl of Manchester, Oliver Cromwell and Henry Ireton

Parliament banners | Commanders

Civil War timeline (1)

1642	
Prince Rupert of the Rhine, Charles's nephew, joins him at Nottingham	July
Standard raised. Earl of Sussex (Parliament) leaves London with untrained army, his coffin and winding sheet	August 22
First skirmish at Powick Bridge	September 23: Royalist victory
King marches to London with over 13,000 men. Occupies slope called Edgehill which dominates road to Banbury, Oxford and London	October
Battle of Edgehill. On road to London, Essex overtakes King. Essex's army plus trained bands form outside city. Badly outnumbered, King retreats to Oxford	October 29: Draw
Cavalry needs fodder; campaigning suspended in winter months	Winter months
1643	
Battle of Braddock Down	January 19: Royalist victory
Essex's advance to Oxford halted by lightning raids of Rupert. Powerful Royalist force threatens Bristol. Earl of Newcastle occupies most of Yorkshire	January to March
Battle of Stratton	May 16: Royalist victory
Battle of Lansdown Heath	July 5: Royalist victory
Battle of Roundway Down	July 13: Royalist victory
Rupert captures Bristol	July 26: Royalist victory
King lays siege to Gloucester	August
Essex leaves London to save Gloucester	September 5: Parliament victory
Returns to hero's welcome. Essex and Charles at first Battle of Newbury	September 20: Draw
King takes Reading	September 18: Royalist victory
Pym enters agreement with Scots. In return for payment and establishment of Presbyterian Church in England, Scots join Parliament side	September
Death of Pym	December 8

▲ Areas controlled by the King and by Parliament, 1642

▲ Areas controlled by the King and by Parliament, 1643

'Monarchy, the best of Governments'

'Long live the King'

'For the King'

Charles I, Sir Ralph Hopton, Prince Rupert, Lord George Goring, Marquis of Montrose, Duke of Newcastle

Royalist banners

Commanders

Civil War timeline (2)

	1644
King orders Lord Deputy in Ireland to make peace with Irish rebels and recruit an army	Spring
Rupert secures ports ready for invasion. Scots join with Fairfax and Manchester and 25,000 Parliament troops lay siege to York. Marquis of Newcastle trapped at York	May
Rupert saves York without shot being fired. Marquis, upset because of off-hand treatment by Rupert, fails to appear for next battle	Royalist victory
Decisive Battle of Marston Moor. Success of Cromwell's Ironsides	July 2: Scottish and Parliament victory
Montrose inflicts six defeats on Covenanters	August: Royalist victories
Second Battle of Newbury	October 27: Draw
Serious quarrels between Manchester and Cromwell. Manchester loses enthusiasm for war. Self-Denying Ordinance – no life peers allowed command in army	December
Cromwell organises New Model Army	Winter
	1645
Negotiations with Irish rebels break down. Serious unrest among common people caused disruption to harvests and markets, pillaging, forced loans, and billeting of troops. Clubmen formed to defend themselves from both sides	January to March
Cromwell and Fairfax meet with large armies	June
At Battle of Naseby New Model Army shows strength. Royalist confidence undermined	June 14: Parliament victory
Goring routed at Langport. Rupert in desperate defence of Bristol	July 10: New Model Army victory
Montrose, after six defeats on Covenanter armies, marches to England	August: Royalist victories
Rupert surrenders Bristol after siege of three weeks	September 20: Parliament victory
Montrose defeated at Philiphaugh	September: Scottish victory
Royalist strongholds surrender. The south-west falls	Winter: Parliament victories
Charles moves from garrison to garrison, avoiding capture	

▲ Areas controlled by the King and by Parliament, 1644

▲ Areas controlled by the King and by Parliament, 1645

'Truly England and the Church of God hath had a great favour from the Lord.' (Marston Moor, 1644)

'God made them as stubble to our swords.'

'This was the mercy of God.' (Oxford, 1645)

'And to see this – is it not to see the face of God?' (Langport, 1645)

Cromwell's writings after victories

'New Noddle'

What was 'New Noddle'?

It was the dismissive nickname given by Royalists to Cromwell's New Model Army, which he formed in the winter of 1644.

What was new about it?

It was the first truly professional army in England.

The army of 22,000 men included the Ironsides, Cromwell's regiment of carefully recruited and trained 'godly men'. The men were well equipped and promptly paid from a central fund. Troops were well disciplined and punishments were severe. Men were whipped for swearing, tongues were bored for blasphemy and the death penalty given for threatening an officer or hitting a civilian. As with the Ironsides, Cromwell paid great attention to their religious training.

Was Cromwell very religious?

As a younger man Cromwell had experienced an intense spiritual feeling which led him to give himself as a devout Puritan to God.

▲ The Battle of Naseby

He was an Independent who demanded freedom of worship and disliked the strictness of the Presbyterians and Church of England. He believed all his victories in battle were God's doing. After the Battle of Naseby in 1645, a decisive Parliamentarian victory, he wrote, 'This was none other than the hand of God and to Him alone belongs the glory.'

Naseby proved to be the last major battle of the war, though fighting did continue. At the last field army battle at Stow-on-the-Wold, the Royalist commander said to his captors, 'You may go and play, unless you fall out among yourselves.'

In April 1646 Charles surrendered to the Scots. When he refused to help them establish the Presbyterian religion in England, they handed him over to Parliament.

The war was over but the falling out had indeed only just begun.

eads of Proposals:	Agreement of the People:
eligious freedom for all except Catholics	Complete religious toleration
eturn to bishops and prayer book	No bishops
arliamentary elections every two years	Parliamentary elections every two years
ouncil of State appointed by army	Absolute power to Parliament
	Vote to all 'freeborn' Englishmen including servants

647 October–November: Putney debates

Crisis

Why did Parliament fall out with its own army?

The Presbyterians in Parliament kept their promise to the Scots. Christmas, Easter, cathedrals, bishops and the Book of Common Prayer were all abolished in England.

The many Independents (Dissenters) in the army, including Cromwell, disliked this strict regime. Matters came to a head when Parliament decided to disband part of the army without granting arrears of pay. The army refused to obey orders and appointed 'Agitators' to negotiate their case.

Cromwell decided to support the army. With his knowledge, the army seized the King, holding him at Newmarket. They then occupied London and expelled 11 Presbyterians from Parliament.

Cromwell and his generals offered Charles new terms for him to reign under the Heads of Proposals in July 1647. It kept the office of King. Charles refused to sign. The Agitators put forward alternative terms in their Agreement of the People. The office of King was not mentioned.

Cromwell was alarmed, and, when the proposals were discussed at Putney, he urged restraint.

▲ A cartoon to persuade Dissenters (left) to agree with Presbyterians

Why was he so alarmed?

The Agitators had become influenced by a group called the Levellers, led by John Lilburne. They called for genuinely revolutionary changes in society and government, with more power to the common people.

As a landowner and gentleman, Cromwell thought only those who owned property should run the country. He and other generals felt that the Levellers were trying to 'raise the servant against the master'. Later, mutinies inspired by the Levellers were harshly put down.

Meanwhile, in the middle of this crisis, Charles escaped to the Isle of Wight.

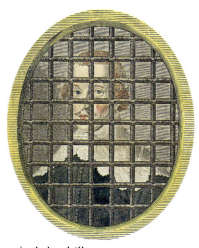

▲ John Lilburne

73

Charles's Engagement with the Scots	Battle of Preston: Royalist defeat	Pride's Purge: expulsion of Presbyterian members	Rump Parliament of about 50 members	Trial of King Charles I	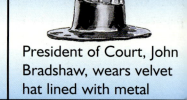 President of Court, John Bradshaw, wears velvet hat lined with metal
1647 December 26	1648 August 17–19	December 6–7		1649 January 20	

'Man of blood'

Charles was held prisoner at Carisbrooke Castle on the Isle of Wight. Within weeks he had signed an 'Engagement', an agreement with the Scots.

What did Charles do?

▲ Charles as prisoner

In return for their military aid, he agreed to establish Presbyterianism in England for three years and to oppose the opinions and practices of the Independents. The Scots marched south in support of Charles for a second Civil War. Their army outnumbered Cromwell's New Model Army by two to one, but they were defeated at a three-day battle around Preston in August 1648. Other Royalist risings in Kent, Essex and Wales were stamped out. Charles was now, after all his dishonesty and double-dealings, 'a man of blood'.

When it was discovered that he had entered an agreement with Parliament to become a Presbyterian monarch, the army generals decided to get rid both of Parliament and King.

Musketeers led by Colonel Pride entered the House of Commons. There, the Colonel 'purged' Parliament by expelling some 100 Presbyterian members and throwing about 50 objectors in prison. After Pride's Purge, the remainder of some 50 members (the 'Rump') was left to represent the people of England. This Rump set up a 'court' of 135 commissioners to try the King. Both the House of Lords and the judges, however, refused to acknowledge it.

On the day of the trial, January 20 1649, only about 85 of the 135 commissioners attended. Cromwell, seeing Charles walking through the garden to Westminster Palace for his trial, exclaimed, 'He is come, he is come, and now we are doing the great work that the whole nation will be full of'.

▲ The trial of Charles I

old and nowing	Charles wears two shirts lest people think he trembles from fear not cold	'I fear not death.'	The Banqueting Hall, Whitehall	Executioner and assistant wear false hair and beards	Death	Handkerchiefs dipped in blood and locks of hair taken	Pamphlets foster memory of royal martyr
649 January 30		10 am			2 pm		

Trial and execution

What was the charge brought against Charles I?

He was accused of responsibility for 'all the treasons, murders, burnings and damages to the nation in the wars'.

He was not allowed to see the charge or defend himself. Charles declared that the king cannot be tried. He demonstrated that the court, carefully chosen by the army, relied on force, not law. He spoke on behalf of his people by arguing that if power without law made laws, 'no subject could be sure of his life or anything he calls his own'.

Cromwell was determined to push through the decision that God had convinced him was the right one.

Fifty-nine commissioners, many of them New Model Army officers, signed the death warrant.

The clerk read out the sentence, 'that the said Charles Stuart, as a Tyrant, Traitor, Murderer and a public enemy, shall be put to death by the severing of his head from his body'.

▲ The execution of King Charles I

Three days later, on January 30 1649, Charles was brought to Whitehall. As he stepped out onto the scaffold, he spoke calmly to those close by. He then stripped off his jewels, the badge of the Order of the Garter and his outer clothing, and tucked his hair into a cap. After kneeling down to pray, he lay down to die. An eyewitness wrote that at the moment of death, 'there was such a groan by the thousands present, as I never heard before and I desire I may never hear again'.

The body of Charles, with the head sewn on, was buried in an unmarked place at Chapel Royal, Windsor. There was no funeral service. Cromwell and the commissioners hoped the King would soon be forgotten.

OLIVER CROMWELL

12

Propaganda in print and pulpit

Was Charles I soon forgotten?

No, because thousands of people were horrified at the manner of his death. Royalist supporters in England and Europe printed masses of propaganda to keep his memory alive.

What is propaganda?

It is information specially designed to give a particular point of view.

▲ The frontispiece of the *Eikon Basilike*

The day after Charles was beheaded, the Royalists printed the *Eikon Basilike – A Portrait of the King*. The frontispiece shows Charles as a Christ-like figure gazing at a heavenly crown. The pamphlet was a runaway best-seller, going through 35 editions in one year. It kept alive the idea of king and monarchy.

In the war of print, the Parliamentarians were at a disadvantage in the 1640s; if they wrote that they were fighting against the King, they risked being tried for treason. Instead they said they were fighting to rescue him from his 'evil advisers'. Pamphlets such as this could show only the King's officers and soldiers being attacked.

In the war of words the Parliamentarians had the advantage of the pulpit. Puritan officers and soldiers of the New Model Army were often preachers. Their Independent ideas spread in many towns and villages.

Both sides printed newspapers from early 1643 but, as Cromwell gained power, censorship increased.

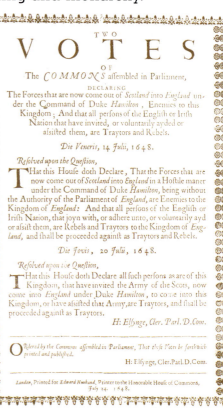

▲ A Parliamentary pamphlet

Rump Parliament	Monarchy abolished	House of Lords abolished	Cromwell lands at Dublin	Siege of Drogheda	Siege of Wexford	Back of resistance broken	Ireland: same system of taxation as England; Irish representatives sat in English Parliament
1648			1649 August	September 11	October		1650 May

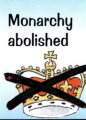

Cromwell and Ireland

Who ruled the country after the death of Charles I?

The Rump continued to rule. It abolished the monarchy and the House of Lords, and declared England a Commonwealth, or 'Republic'.

But there were immediate problems. The Irish Catholics refused to accept the Commonwealth and rose in rebellion. In the summer of 1649 Cromwell took troops of the New Model Army to Ireland where, quickly and efficiently – but with shocking brutality – he defeated them. At the garrison of Drogheda, about 3,000 men and priests, women and children were slaughtered without mercy. Cromwell called it 'a just judgement of God upon those barbarous wretches that have imbrued [stained] their hands in so much innocent blood'.

At Wexford garrison 2,000 men and civilians were also butchered.

▲ The Irish campaign

▲ The Siege of Drogheda

Why did Cromwell commit these atrocities?

The campaign was partly in revenge for the Catholic murders of Protestants in 1641. The innocent blood he referred to was Protestant blood.

Cromwell also claimed that 'it will tend to prevent the effusion [spilling] of blood for the future'. By striking terror into two garrisons, he thought others would surrender. Some garrisons held out gallantly, but resistance was eventually broken. As a result of the defeat, power passed to the Protestants, who then became the ruling class. Indeed, Catholic worship was banned. More than a third of Irish land was confiscated and redistributed to former soldiers and English investors. Irish landowners were forced to move to Connaught in Western Ireland.

Ireland was temporarily united with England – but the Irish did not become English. Hatred between the races continued. Cromwell, meanwhile, returned to a hero's welcome.

Charles II escapes from Worcester	Hidden in Catholic households	Disguised as peasant called Will Jones and skin stained with walnut juice	Spends a day hidden in the Royal Oak	Disguised as lady's servant	Fails to sail from Bristol, Charmouth, Southampton	Blacksmith notices horses shod in fashion of Worcester area	Sails from Shoreham to France

1651 September 3   October 15

Cromwell and Scotland

Cromwell was actually recalled from Ireland to fight the Scots.

Why did he fight fellow Protestants?

The Presbyterian Scots had proclaimed Prince Charles (the eldest son of Charles I) Charles II of Scotland, England and Ireland. In return, Charles promised to establish Presbyterianism in Scotland and England.

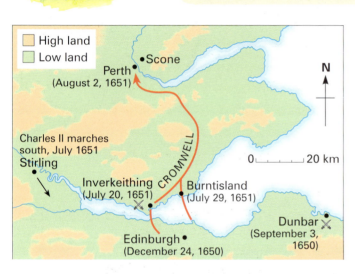

▲ The Scottish campaign

The threat of another Scottish invasion and a possible third Civil War led England to declare war against Scotland on July 4 1650. Fairfax, the Commander-in-Chief, resigned rather than fight against his 'brethren'. Cromwell took his place.

The Scots, meanwhile, still rejected all attempts to reach an agreement. With 22,000 troops to Cromwell's 13,000, they expected an easy victory at the first battle at Dunbar.

After a dawn raid and two hours' fighting, Cromwell lost about 30 men. The Scots lost 3,000.

After battle, the victorious troops of the New Model Army gathered around Cromwell to sing Psalm 117: 'O give praise unto the Lord, All nations that be.'

Charles II, however, was crowned at Scone on New Year's Day 1651.

In July, despite further English victories in Scotland, Charles decided to march into England where he hoped Royalists would join him. Eventually he reached Worcester, but had fewer than 13,000 men. Cromwell commanded 31,000.

The result was inevitable, but Charles escaped to face further adventures. Worcester was Cromwell's last battle in a military career spanning nine years. He had never experienced defeat, and interpreted his victories as a sign from God that he should rule the Commonwealth of Great Britain. He now had to change from a military to a civilian rule.

▲ Charles hides in the Royal Oak, Boscobel

ump arliament	Barebones' Parliament named after a member, Praise-be-to-God Barebones, a London leatherseller	Protectorate: Oliver Cromwell	Richard Cromwell	Rump Parliament	Convention Parliament	Charles II
48–1653	April–December	1653 December–1658 September	1658 September –1659 May	1659	1660	1661 April 23

THE COMMONWEALTH

Interregnum

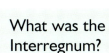

What was the Interregnum?

It is Latin meaning 'between the reigns' and marks the years when Cromwell was in power.

▲ 'Begone, you rogues, you have sat long enough!'

During these years he tried several experiments in Parliamentary government. By 1653 Cromwell had become impatient at the Rump's failure to carry out reforms. He dismissed this 'Long Parliament' by using force: twenty musketeers with loaded weapons waited outside the Chamber while Cromwell marched up and down shouting abuse at the members. He picked up the Mace, the symbol of the Speaker's authority, and ordered 'the bauble' be taken away. The musketeers helped him to clear the House.

The next experiment, Barebones' Parliament, lasted only six months: the 140 nominated god-fearing men – the 'Assembly of Saints' – failed to agree.

▲ Lord Protector, Oliver Cromwell

The next plan invented a new title for Cromwell. Wearing a black velvet cloak and in a simple ceremony at Westminster Abbey, he was installed as Lord Protector. He moved to Whitehall, the usual residence of the monarch. His first Parliament objected to his king-like powers, so this was dismissed. Then, after a Royalist rising, he decided to experiment with army rule alone.

In 1655 he divided the country into 11 districts, each governed by a Major-General. They were there for the 'suppression of vice' and the 'encouragement of virtue', in line with Cromwell's religious views.

Almost overnight many 'pleasures' were suppressed. Bear-baiting, cock-fighting and gambling were forbidden, and public houses and theatres were closed. This military rule was deeply resented and his Second Protectorate Parliament wanted change. They presented Cromwell with the Humble Petition and Advice. One clause, in fact, offered him the crown of England.

79

King Oliver I?

Did Cromwell accept the crown?

After weeks of agonising over his decision, he answered, 'I am ready to serve not as a king, but as a constable... a good constable to keep the peace of the parish.' He could not 'find it his duty to God and Parliament to undertake this charge under that title'.

▲ A Dutch cartoon of Cromwell of about 1658

It has to be said that many men in the army would probably have objected to the title of 'king' too.

In May a second petition, which omitted the title of king, was presented. Cromwell accepted this, and on June 26 1657 he was reinvested as Lord Protector at Whitehall.

On this occasion he wore a purple velvet cloak lined with ermine. He swore an oath, and accepted a sword of state and a sceptre of gold.

The Humble Petition had advised the setting up of a new House of Lords. Cromwell did this, and filled it with supporters of the government. The Commons, however, were bitterly opposed to this 'other House'. Thus Cromwell dissolved Parliament.

By 1658 Cromwell was old and ill. Financial problems had become severe and his regime had become unpopular. On September 3 1658 he died. His body lay in state for eight weeks and he was given a magnificent state funeral at Westminster Abbey.

His nominated successor, his son Richard, received little support and resigned in 1659. In May 1660, one of Cromwell's commanders, General Monck, occupied London and declared for a free Parliament. This supported the return of Charles II, who was eager to reclaim his crown.

Charles II

What was the general feeling when a king was restored to the throne?

When Charles II entered London on May 29 1660, it was a time of great rejoicing.

John Evelyn – an eyewitness – wrote of 'the triumph of above 20,000 horse and foot, brandishing their swords and shouting with inexpressible joy; the ways strewed with flowers, the bells ringing, the streets hung with tapestry, fountains running with wine'.

After his coronation on April 23 1661, the King continued in the same tone of gaiety and pleasure. Theatres which had been closed for 18 years were re-opened and his subjects saw him there, laughing at amusing and sometimes vulgar plays. He rode, danced, enjoyed tennis, discussed state affairs between matches, played with his favourite spaniel dogs, sailed his yacht, gambled and enjoyed the company of many mistresses before and after marriage.

His wife, Catherine of Braganza, daughter of the King of Portugal, brought a large dowry of £300,000 cash, the island of Bombay, the port of Tangier and valuable trading privileges for English seamen in the New World.

▲ Catherine of Braganza, Charles's wife

Charles's people, perhaps understandably, reacted to the restrictions of the long period under the Puritans by enjoying pastimes long denied by Cromwell. Card-playing and gambling, musical entertainments, reading news-sheets, and visits to taverns and coffee-houses, became popular once more.

▲ The coronation procession of Charles II

A 'hack' was an old or poor breed of horse

Horseback   Hackney coach   Sedan chair

London in 1664

If a fashionable visitor spent the day in London in around 1664, what would it have been like?

A Restoration gentleman like that would have been visiting the largest city in Europe and probably the noisiest, most congested, and the most stinking!

He might start his day by visiting an ale house or tavern to drink a morning draught of beer or wine, play cards and smoke tobacco.

He could buy his tobacco from Mr Farr's shop, 'The Best Tobacco by Farr', or from Mr Farr's rival's shop, 'Far Better Tobacco than the Best Tobacco by Farr'.

He might prefer to visit Bowman's coffee-house at Cornhill or the Rainbow in Fleet Street. It cost a penny to enter, and inside he could gossip and read newspapers whilst drinking coffee or chocolate. He could order food, write letters and arrange to receive mail. Stepping outside he would be met with the endless cries of street vendors – 'Fair cherryes!', 'Buy my flounders!', 'Smallcoale!', 'Dish of great eeles!'.

▲ A Restoration gentleman

▲ A London coffee-house in 1668

As for shops, they provided specialist goods. He could buy shoes in Cordwainer Street, books in Fleet Street, a mirror in Glass House Alley or trinkets in Silver Street. In Smithfield he would need to look out for the drunken drovers running with the cattle for fun through the streets. The poor animals would sometimes take refuge in the shops!

Triangular gallows	Last mug of ale for condemned prisoners	Prisoners dress like bridegrooms or in mourning	Cart stopped under cross-beam of gibbet	Horse lashed, cart moves, victim swings	Relatives pull on legs and beat breast to speed up death	Hangman takes clothes and sells pieces of rope

burn

A fascinating city

If the gentleman should stroll down Pall Mall, he might see King Charles playing the game of pell mell with one of his mistresses.

In the afternoon he could go to the Theatre Royal in Drury Lane.

If it was a public holiday he might join a crowd of around 12,000 people at Tyburn to enjoy a different kind of spectacle. There, up to 20 convicted criminals could be hanged at the same time on the triangular scaffold.

▲ One form of 'pell mell'

Ugh! A public execution on a public holiday!

The sight of an execution was supposed to act as a deterrent.

After that, a boat trip across the River Thames would take him to the Bear Gardens to see cock fights, dog fights, bear- or bull-baiting. There the bull might toss the dog up high into his lap!

How horrible!

A walk in Vauxhall Gardens would be quieter. There, he could listen to the nightingales, the music of fiddles and harp, and take refreshments.

He would be advised to leave London before dark as there could be many rogues and vagabonds lurking in the streets.

If he did linger into the evening, he could hire a link boy with a torch to guide his way past the dunghills, potholes and drunken brawls. If he stayed the night at an inn, he might hear the nightwatchman call out 'past three o'clock on a warm summer morning'.

▲ Watermen ferrying gentlefolk across the River Thames

But he would not have visited London in the summer of 1665; the streets were deathly quiet. Indeed, the only street cry he would have heard was 'Bring out your dead! Bring out your dead!'

'Ring-a-ring-a-roses'

'Rings' were soft, black swellings
'Roses' were pink-coloured rashes

'A pocketful of posies'

Herbs, spices and perfumes to ward off the stench of death

'Tishoo, tishoo'

Sneezing was a common symptom of approaching death

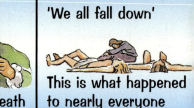
'We all fall down'

This is what happened to nearly everyone

This nursery rhyme is associated with the plague

THE PLAGUE
14 London in 1665

Why were so many people dying in 1665?

They were victims of the plague.

▲ A map of London in the 1660s

Ever since the time of the Black Death in 1348, it was the disease that English people feared the most. They knew that, once caught, the outcome was usually death. Outbreaks of the plague continued through Tudor and Stuart times and, in 1625, over 40,000 people in London died of it.

You can see from the map how small London was in the 17th century. It was not much more than a mile long from one end to the other. By 1665, a population of about 460,000 lived within the city walls. Outside the walls, settlements with their own parish churches were well-established. These parishes tended to house the poor in over-crowded slum conditions.

London within the walls was a dirty, infested city. The streets were narrow, with old wooden houses which had been built close together, and the air was grimy with smoke from the many coal fires. Filthy rubbish, such as offal from butchers' shops, was thrown onto the streets and into the River Fleet which flowed alongside the city walls. Water was drawn from this river to pumps and fountains in the city. There were no public toilets. It was not surprising that people caught infectious diseases. The city council realised that there was a connection between dirt and disease, and ordered rubbish collections, but as yet no one understood the link between rats, fleas and disease.

▲ London was an ideal breeding ground for the rats which came from trading-boats on the River Thames

You mean nothing had changed since medieval times!

 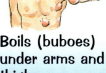   

Victims became weak and dizzy	Boils (buboes) under arms and thighs	These grow as large as apples or onions	Sweating and fever	Black spots or blotches spread over body	Vomiting and spitting blood	Cannot swallow water	About two-thirds of victims dead within a week

Symptoms of plague

Plague takes hold

The plague was first reported in the winter of 1664 in the poor, over-crowded parish of St Giles-in-the-Field, which was outside the city walls. By early 1665 between 3,000 and 4,000 people were reported as dying each week. King Charles II was at this time in Oxford, but in March, when deaths were reported as declining, he and his family returned to their residence at Whitehall. Londoners who had left for safety in the country also returned.

When did this outbreak start?

So, they thought it was over – but was it?

No. By the end of March, when the weather became warmer, deaths rose dramatically.

▲ Burying the victims of the plague

The numbers of dead were reported weekly in a Bill of Mortality and, towards the end of March, 6,000 people were recorded as having died from the plague. Some observers estimated a far higher figure of 14,000 deaths. The plague then began to appear within the city walls. By June and July the King and court left for Surrey, and then Oxford, where Parliament was held.

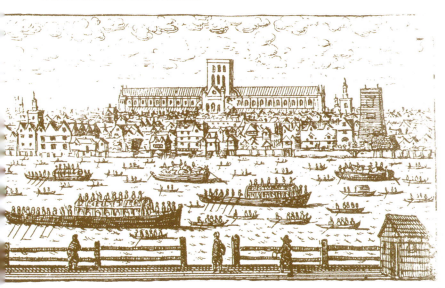

▲ People left in carriages, coaches, waggons, carts, on horseback and by boat

Thousands became refugees and fled in fear from the city. The watermen, who ferried boats, moved their own families upriver. There they camped by day, making tents from the sails, and at night they slept on hay in the boats.

A Dr Vincent wrote 'and a deep silence is almost every place, especially within the walls; no rattling coaches, no prancing horses, no calling in customers, nor offering wares, no London-cryes sounding in the ears'.

By August of that year, London was as quiet as the grave.

4p a corpse

Searchers

2p an animal

Cat and dog killer

Corpse bearers

Burial carts

'Bring out your dead'

Hand bells rung

People would not buy wigs in case the hair came from plague victims

Wigs

Emergency measures

If the plague was so deadly, what precautions were taken?

▲ A watchman keeping guard

Victims and their families were confined to their homes and a watchman posted outside to make sure only a doctor and nurses could enter and families did not try to leave. Some people escaped only to spread the disease. Infected houses were closed for 40 days after the sick had died or recovered.

A high-ranking civil servant, Samuel Pepys, who knew King Charles well, kept a personal diary.

He noted on June 7 that he had seen, for the first time, houses with red crosses marked on doors and 'Lord have mercy upon us' written there. At first, people were buried in graveyards, but these filled so rapidly that huge 'plague pits', which could take up to 400 bodies, were dug in fields outside the city walls.

The number of dead in the Bill of Mortality for the last week of August was recorded at 6,102, but Pepys thought that the true number was nearer to 10,000.

Emergency measures were introduced. For example, people had to clean the streets in front of their houses, bonfires had to be lit to purify the air, and cats and dogs were to be killed.

But it was rats which spread the disease!

Yes, but that was not known then. People spent a fortune on ridiculous cures. One remedy advised taking a pigeon or hen, plucking out the tail feathers and pressing the tail on the swelling. The venom in the body of the victim was meant to pass into the bird, which would then die. Some brave doctors, who stayed in London, scorned these remedies. Most doctors and priests, however, left the city.

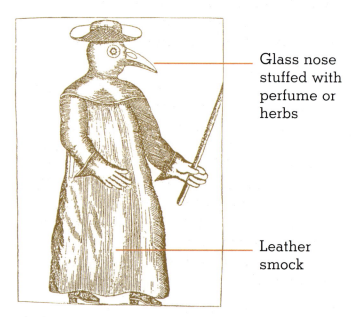

Glass nose stuffed with perfume or herbs

Leather smock

▲ Some doctors wore a rather alarming costume like this when they visited people with the plague

3 deaths	267 deaths	470 deaths	1,843 deaths	2,817 deaths	6,102 deaths	6,978 deaths
665 June 6	June 27	July 4	July 21	August 8	August 29	September 5
.165 deaths	4,929 deaths	1,421 deaths	1,414 deaths	337 deaths	210 deaths	281 deaths
eptember 19	October 3	October 14	November 7	November 26	December 5	December 19

Deaths from the plague, as recorded in the weekly Bills of Mortality

Deaths decline

On September 4 1665, Pepys wrote in a letter that the Bill of Mortality had recorded the deaths of 6,000 people that week. He mentioned whole families of 10 to 12 people who had been wiped out, as well as the deaths of his own physician, his baker, and his baker's whole family. Later, he wrote of others he knew who had died: one of his ferrymen, his waiter whose child had died, a labourer, and the fathers of two of his servants.

How could they count every dead person?

That was not possible. The weekly figures for the Bill of Mortality were collected by 'searchers of the dead'.

The gruesome job of these searchers (old women) was to check corpses and determine the cause of death. The searchers reported their numbers to the parish clerk, but clerks and gravediggers died too, and thousands of other victims were buried in unknown graves in gardens and fields. Some searchers took bribes to disguise the cause of death. Historians can only estimate the actual number of dead.

A decline in deaths was eventually reported in November and the King and his court returned to the city after Christmas. London slowly came to life again. Estimates put deaths in London at about 100,000. A chaplain who saw official reports estimated 200,000 deaths in England as a whole. He wrote 'and I hope and pray that God will never send the like and that we nor our posterity after us may never feel such another judgement'.

But, just as Londoners were recovering from this catastrophe, they were struck by another.

The Diseases and Casualties this Week.

			Imposthume	11
			Infants	16
			Killed by a fall from the Belfrey at Alhallows the Great	1
			Kingsevil	2
			Lethargy	1
			Palsie	1
			Plague	7165
Abortive	5		Rickets	17
Aged	43		Rising of the Lights	11
Ague	2		Scowring	5
Apoplexie	1		Scurvy	2
Bleeding	2		Spleen	1
Burnt in his Bed by a Candle at St. Giles Cripplegate	1		Spotted Feaver	101
Canker	1		Stilborn	17
Childbed	42		Stone	2
Chrisomes	18		Stopping of the stomach	9
Consumption	134		Strangury	1
Convulsion	64		Suddenly	1
Cough	2		Surfeit	49
Dropsie	33		Teeth	121
Feaver	309		Thrush	5
Flox and Small-pox	5		Timpany	1
Frighted	3		Tissick	11
Gowt	1		Vomiting	3
Grief	3		Winde	3
Griping in the Guts	51		Wormes	15
Jaundies	5			

Christned { Males — 95, Females — 81, In all — 176 }
Buried { Males — 4095, Females — 4202, In all — 8297 } Plague — 7165

Increased in the Burials this Week — 607
Parishes clear of the Plague — 4   Parishes Infected — 126

The Assize of Bread set forth by Order of the Lord Maior and Court of Aldermen, A penny Wheaten Loaf to contain Nine Ounces and a half, and three half-penny White Loaves the like weight.

▲ The Bill of Mortality for the week of September 12–19

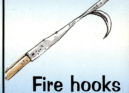
1666 Sunday, September 2

Fire

In the early hours of Sunday, September 2 1666, Thomas Farriner, a baker who lived with his family above their shop in Pudding Lane, was woken by the smell of smoke and the sound of crackling timber. A downstairs oven had overheated and caught fire. Thomas, his wife and daughter, escaped through an upstairs window. Their maidservant, who refused to leave, perished in the flames.

From this small fire a huge blaze spread, devastating the heart of the city of London and causing distress and financial ruin to thousands of Londoners.

How was it that the whole of London caught fire?

The flames spread rapidly because of a strong, east wind which was blowing at the time. Sparks from the baker's shop set fire to some stables attached to an inn on Fish Hill Street near London Bridge.

▲ A dramatic painting of the fire of London

Once the hay and straw caught fire, the embers were blown onto the inn itself. The wind drove the flames through the narrow alleys and overhanging houses until they reached large sheds and warehouses down by the River Thames. Once the inflammable materials of tar, oil, timber and other goods were set ablaze, the fire became unstoppable.

By 8am, Pepys saw burning houses at the end of London Bridge which prevented people from escaping by that route. He probably saw that the intensity of the heat had melted lead water pipes and destroyed water wheels. He knew that there was little water and inadequate fire-fighting equipment to fight such an immense fire. As people fled, Pepys hastened to inform the King at Whitehall.

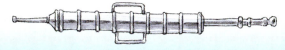
London's burning

On Pepys's advice, King Charles ordered that buildings in the path of the fire should be pulled down.

This was done by throwing fire hooks attached to ropes onto the sides of buildings. Men or horses pulling on the ropes would then bring down the buildings.

The problem was that the spread of fire was so rapid that flames leapt and licked at the debris of timber, plaster and thatch. Fanned by the east wind, it kept on raging.

Landowners paid huge sums of money for carts to carry away their possessions. Sick relatives, still in their beds, were moved, and people fled in boats and barges to safety. There was panic and chaos and a feeling of utter helplessness in the face of the fire. Thousands of homeless people camped in fields outside the city walls.

Businessmen hid goods in cellars or buried them in gardens. Stationers and booksellers near St Paul's Cathedral, thinking it safe, stored their goods inside. On Tuesday evening embers were blown onto scaffolding and onto the roof. Londoners watched in disbelief as their much-loved place of worship burst into flames and was reduced to ashes.

One observer saw lead on the roof oozing down 'as if it had been snow before the sun'. John Evelyn, a diarist, noted the 'fiery rednesse of the pavement and the melting lead running down the streets in a streame so that no horse or man was able to tread on them'. Another onlooker read his book by the brilliant light of the fire.

What did the King do?

▲ Fire hooks being used –
a picture by a modern artist

▲ St Paul's Cathedral is destroyed in the fire

89

Fetch the engines

How was the fire brought under control?

Thousands of Londoners did their best to contain the blaze. Even King Charles and his brother James, the Duke of York, helped by manning fire engines and giving orders to clear away buildings.

The King feared that the fire might spread to the Tower of London, causing the gunpowder there to explode. If this happened, London Bridge would be destroyed, boats sunk and widespread damage would result. To avoid this, he ordered that houses near the ditch surrounding the Tower should be demolished, and also those near Whitehall and Westminster Abbey. At last, at about 4 o'clock on the Tuesday afternoon, the wind dropped. It rose again during the evening but died down at last on the Wednesday.

Buildings continued to burn and the heat of the ground was such that it burnt the soles of Evelyn's shoes. Smoke and stench filled the air for days and, even when the cellars were opened the following March, Pepys noticed smoke breaking out again!

The King commanded that food supplies should be brought to London, made sure that possessions were guarded and visited the homeless. People gradually returned to their everyday lives again.

How much of London was destroyed?

▲ London immediately after the fire

Look at this map of the time, which shows the extent of the devastation.

Miraculously, hardly anyone had died, but it was estimated that in addition to St Paul's Cathedral and some chapels, 89 parish churches and 13,200 houses had been destroyed. Numerous warehouses were destroyed and some merchants lost fortunes.

Principal architect for rebuilding of London	Designed hospitals at Chelsea, Greenwich and Royal Exchange		Designed churches, including St Brides in Fleet Street	Plans drawn up for St Paul's Cathedral	Became president of the Royal Society	Si Monumentum Requiris Circumspice ('If you seek his monument, look around you')
Sir Christopher Wren (1632–1723)				1673	1680	Tomb inscription

Phoenix from the ashes

Weren't people insured, so that they would receive some compensation for what they had lost?

Fire insurance did not exist then, but gradually fire insurance firms were set up. People paid small sums of money and, if a fire did occur, these firms would send out their own fire-brigades.

Was the city completely redesigned?

Many ideas were put forward to create a new town plan, including some by Sir Christopher Wren, a brilliant architect who was also a mathematician, astronomer and scientist.

As people preferred to build on the old street plans and as quickly as possible, all schemes were rejected.

Wren, however, became principal architect for a new London. His first task was to design a monument in memory of the Great Fire. He went on to create wonderful buildings including hospitals, colleges and more than 50 churches.

The most famous church was the new St Paul's Cathedral. This took 35 years to build and Wren is buried there. If you climb the stone steps to the Stone gallery outside the dome, you can see the spires and towers of Wren's churches and the Monument 'neere unto the place where the said Fire soe unhappily began'. By 1672 a new London had risen from the ashes.

How was it so different?

All new houses had to be built of brick or stone. Carpets and panelling inside houses replaced straw and cloth hangings. Fleas and rats were deprived of a home. The streets were wider, common sewers and fresher water were provided. It was a cleaner and healthier city. Never again was there a plague or fire on such a scale as those in 1665 and 1666 respectively.

▲ The Monument and London after its rebuilding

Founding of the Royal Society for the Promotion of Natural Knowledge	Robert Boyle, founder of modern chemistry, discovered that air is made up of different elements	Samuel Pepys, Christopher Wren, John Evelyn, Isaac Newton	Robert Hooke used his microscope to study phenomena, such as plant cells, which were unknown to man
1660 Famous members			**About 1680**

THE BIRTH OF MODERN SCIENCE

16

Challenging accepted beliefs

Christopher Wren played an important part in setting up the Royal Society, which was granted a charter by Charles II in 1662. The idea of the Society grew from a group of Englishmen who had met regularly since 1645 to investigate topics such as navigation, architecture, agriculture, medicine and science.

Where did they get the idea to form such a group?

It was the Renaissance movement – the rebirth of interest in the arts and science, which had begun in the 14th century and was still flourishing – that encouraged these men to reach out and search for new knowledge.

By questioning and experimenting, they began to challenge accepted scientific ideas of Greek philosophers such as Aristotle.

What were his ideas?

He had so many, but as an example of one that was challenged, he believed that the earth was a solid sphere fixed in the centre of the universe.

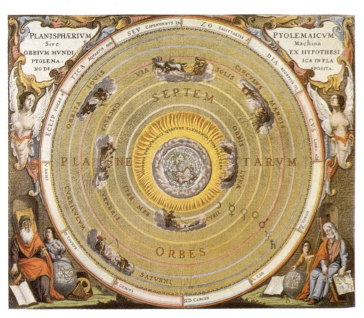

▲ Ptolemy's universe – the sun and planets circle the earth

▲ Copernicus's universe – planets, including the earth, circle the sun

Ptolemy, a 2nd-century Greek scholar, based his ideas on Aristotle, and belief in these ideas lasted until the 16th century. In 1543 a Polish scholar, Copernicus, published his belief that the planets revolve round the sun.

Other scholars, such as Brahe (a Dane), Kepler (a German) and Galileo (an Italian), contributed to man's new understanding of the universe. Galileo – who believed that the sun and not the earth was the centre of the universe and that the earth moved – was forbidden by the Catholic Church to hold, teach or defend his views, which were considered 'foolish and absurd'.

The Royal Society encouraged scientists and their experiments. Men's ideas of God and their scientific understanding were gradually changing.

| oundation tone laid | Charles II appoints Astronomer Royal to work out position of Greenwich and various stars | Sailors anywhere in world can observe stars and work out position compared with Greenwich | Greenwich meridian still base-line for world maps |

675 Greenwich Royal Observatory

Sir Isaac Newton

One outstanding member of the Royal Society, and acknowledged as such today, was Sir Isaac Newton, a scientist. By learning from and building on the work of earlier astronomers, he was eventually able to demonstrate how the strength of the force of gravity held the solar system together.

The story goes that the fall of an apple led him towards this discovery.

How on earth did a falling apple help?

It helped because it landed on earth! Newton wondered why some objects are pulled towards the earth and others, like the moon, are not.

▲ Sir Isaac Newton

He proposed the theory that the moon falls like an apple, but because of the speed and the course of the earth, the two never meet. No matter whether it is a cannon ball, a planet, an orange, the tides of a sea or a human being, they are all controlled by the same gravitational forces.

Nor was this theory the sum of his life's work. He went on to prove more earth-shattering theories:

- He invented the reflecting telescope which used a concave mirror.
- Using a prism, he broke white light into the seven colours of the spectrum – red, orange, yellow, green, blue, indigo and violet.
- He introduced a new type of mathematics called Calculus.
- He wrote a famous book, *Principia Mathematica*, which helped scientists all over the world to understand the universe.

He remarked 'but to myself I seem to have been only a boy playing on the seashore... whilst the great ocean of truth lay all undiscovered before me'.

Like Shakespeare, Newton was a genius of the Renaissance and a genius for all time.

Aristotle and the human body	Four 'humours':	Associated with:	Corresponded to stages in life:	Led to human personalities:	Body and soul (microcosm) reflect universe (macrocosm)
	Blood	Spring	Childhood	Sanguine (high spirited)	
	Yellow bile	Summer	Youth	Choleric (bad tempered)	
	Black bile	Autumn	Maturity	Melancholy	
	Phlegm	Winter	Old age	Phlegmatic	

Aristotle

Medicine

Did Aristotle hold medical as well as scientific beliefs?

He did indeed. He thought there was a connection between the universe and the human body.

He believed that the universe was made up of four elements – earth, air, fire and water. Because of the movements of the planets, there was a constant battle between these elements. He believed that the human body was made up of four 'humours' – blood, yellow bile, black bile and phlegm. The human body reflected the struggles between the elements, as the four humours were conflicting ones. All illness was thought to be a lack of balance between the humours.

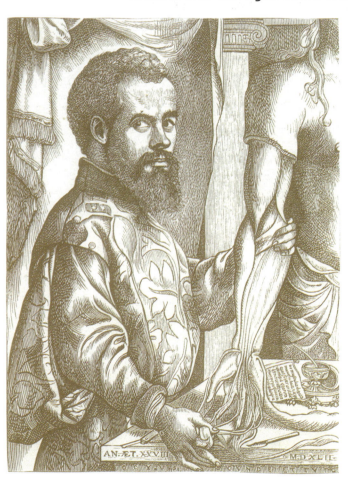

▲ Andreas Vesalius, aged 28, from *The Fabric of the Human Body*

So, if I was too lively and high spirited, what could be done?

Your 'humour' was blood, so you could be bled and this would restore harmony to your body.

It sounds an extraordinary theory to me!

Perhaps, but remember that Aristotle was alive in the 4th century BC! It was an ingenious theory based on the knowledge available at that time.

It was the Renaissance movement that encouraged physicians to rely more on careful observations and dissection of human bodies to provide new theories and reach new conclusions.

In 1543 a professor of surgery and anatomy at Padua in Italy, Andreas Vesalius, published a book called *The Fabric of the Human Body*. It changed people's knowledge of the structure of the human body.

Vesalius drew most of the illustrations and worked with a painter on others. Not only physicians but Renaissance artists, such as Leonardo da Vinci, Michelangelo, Raphael and Titian, also studied skeletons and dissected bodies in order to improve their understanding of their subject.

reatment of ounds by ouring boiling il on them	Simple dressings and bandages	Red-hot cautery iron to stop bleeding	Ligature (tying of artery)	Prescriptions made from mummies and unicorns	Investigations by Paré declare them useless
ld	New	Old	New	Old	New

Further advances

In 1575 another important medical text, *Works on Surgery*, by a French army surgeon called Ambroise Paré, changed understanding about how to treat gunshot wounds and amputations. Paré discovered that gunshot wounds did not contain 'poison' as previously thought, and that they could be treated with a soothing dressing rather than boiling oil. Instead of using the barbaric cautery iron to stop the bleeding after an amputation, he experimented and advised the use of a ligature.

He devised several forms of artificial limbs to replace amputated ones.

In 1628 another book, *On the Movement of the Heart and the Blood*, furthered knowledge on physiology (the study of how the living body works). The author, an Englishman called William Harvey, proved it was the heart, rather than the liver, that was the central blood organ in the body. The heart, acting as a pump, moved the same blood in one direction round the body.

Was his work recognised immediately?

No. He was regarded as 'crackbrained' and he thought that his livelihood was ruined.

▲ Using a cautery iron

It took time for these discoveries to affect everyday life. People still clung to old superstitions and cures.

Some cures, such as powdered unicorn horn, were nonsense. Others, like quinine, are still used today. The herb tobacco was supposed to expel worms from the stomach, ease griping pains, kill head lice and expel phlegm. Its ashes were used to cleanse the gums and make teeth white.

One thing tobacco certainly did was to make a profit. By 1671 Virginia tobacco had made £100,000 from import duties – a huge sum in those days.

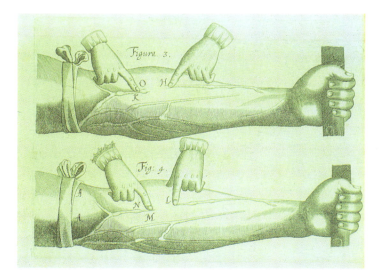

▲ An illustration from Harvey's book demonstrating how valves and veins work

95

Tobacco

Smoking American tobacco in clay pipe

Sugar

Rum

Hudson Bay Company Charter

Muskets   Hatchets   Fur

Growth in trade from American colonies   **1670** May 2

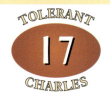

The colonisation of North America

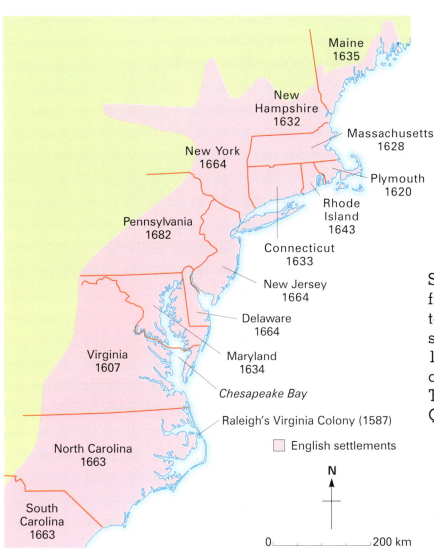

▲ English settlements in North America

Maine 1635
New Hampshire 1632
New York 1664
Massachusetts 1628
Plymouth 1620
Rhode Island 1643
Connecticut 1633
New Jersey 1664
Pennsylvania 1682
Delaware 1664
Virginia 1607
Maryland 1634
Chesapeake Bay
Raleigh's Virginia Colony (1587)
North Carolina 1663
South Carolina 1663

English settlements

N

0 _____ 200 km

Did the tobacco come from the original settlement of Elizabethan times?

Yes, and you can see from the map how, once Virginia prospered, others followed.

Some of these were religious settlements, as freedom to worship was still a reason to sail to the New World. Maryland was a Catholic settlement and Rhode Island was Baptist. In 1681 Charles II granted William Penn a charter to found Pennsylvania (Penn's forest). This was a settlement for persecuted Quakers.

Why did people have to have charters?

Royal permission was needed because, in theory, all land overseas belonged to the King, and subjects were not free to leave England as they wished.

A charter was granted to the Hudson Bay Company, headed by Prince Rupert, in 1670. The English landed in Canadian fur country only because two French sailors who had quarrelled with their governor led them there. Charles allowed this company to trade 'over all regions whose waters empty into Hudson Bay'.

Kings enjoyed the prestige of owning colonies. Such colonies increased the power and wealth of their own 'mother' country. Charles II was entitled to one-fifth of any precious metal found: goods sent to colonies were charged royal custom duties and colonial exports had to come to England first. Goods such as tobacco, sugar and rum were welcomed for the profit they made.

England was gradually adding exotic imports to the unglamorous one of Newfoundland cod.

rporation Act. own Councillors fusing ommunion smissed.	Act of Uniformity. New prayer book.	THE ◄ CLARENDON ► CODE	Conventicle Act. Everyone to attend Church of England services only.	Five Mile Act. No dissenting clergyman or schoolmaster to live nearer than five miles from a town.

61

Tolerance

Did Charles take revenge on the 59 regicides ('killers of kings') who had signed the death warrant of his father, Charles I?

Nine regicides were rounded up and publicly hanged. Many had already fled or had died in prison.

On the 11th anniversary of his father's death, the bodies of Cromwell, Ireton and Bradshaw were dug up, hanged at Tyburn and their heads displayed.

Charles never sought personal revenge. He told his first Cavalier Parliament 'that mercy and indulgence is the best way to bring men to a true repentance'. He pardoned all those who fought against his father and found places at court, in councils and local government for Royalists and Parliamentarians.

Charles was also prepared to be tolerant about religious matters. He tried to restore the position of the Church of England with reforms that would make it acceptable to most Puritans.

His Cavalier Parliament thought otherwise. A series of laws, known as the Clarendon Code, was passed. These laws were rigorously enforced by JPs. For example, the first and second punishments for attending a religious service which was not of the Church of England was prison. The third punishment was transportation. About 2,000 Puritan ministers who refused to use the new prayer book were expelled from their livelihoods. Many dissenting Nonconformists (those who disagreed with the Church of England) left for America. The Puritan Quakers, Baptists, Separatists and Catholics could not share in the government, administration or education system of the country.

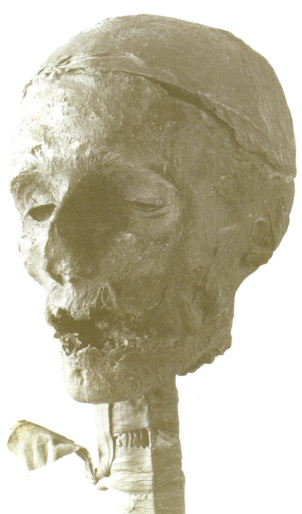

▲ Cromwell's skull

In 1673 Charles, in a Declaration of Indulgence, tried to make it easier for all such 'Nonconformists' to get jobs. MPs were furious.

97

King told by Titus Oates, former Jesuit and Anglican clergyman, that he will be waylaid by Irish ruffians, stabbed by Jesuits, shot with silver bullets and poisoned by Queen's physician. Oates's accusations lead to deaths of about 30 innocent Catholic priests.

1678 September

Another Catholic plot

Why were MPs furious?

They suspected Charles had leanings towards the Catholic faith – he had, in fact, signed a secret treaty with the French, the Treaty of Dover, which hoped to restore the Catholic faith in England.

Charles's mother, brother and sister were all Catholics. MPs were worried because although Charles had 17 children, none of them would be the next Protestant heir to the throne.

Why not?

Because they were all illegitimate! The Crown would therefore go to Charles's brother, James, who had openly become Catholic in 1670.

In 1678 the situation was made worse when rumours spread of a Popish plot to kill the King and replace him with his Catholic brother, James. These playing cards of the time tell the story.

▲ Oates informs the King of the plot

▲ Oates swears his unlikely tale is true before Berry

Titus Oates, an informer, swore the rumours were true in front of a magistrate, Sir Edmund Berry, who was later found murdered. He was rumoured to be the first Protestant victim of the massacre. Multitudes flocked to see the openly displayed body. His funeral was attended by a thousand nobles, clergy and gentry. At about this time, James's secretary, a Catholic, was found with letters to Rome in his possession. These wrote of converting the English throne to Catholicism. All this created real terror and panic in London. Charles, who never believed Oates, was forced by Parliament to call out the militia, fill the prisons with hundreds of Catholics, place cannon round Whitehall and put guards in the same cellar where Guy Fawkes was found.

Charles's main political opponent in Parliament, Lord Shaftesbury, exploited the plot. He formed the Whig party, with the main purpose of attacking the government.

Whigs: Those <u>for</u> getting rid of James II. From word 'whiggamor' meaning 'cattle driver'. Term of abuse for Scottish Presbyterians.

Tories: Those <u>against</u> getting rid of James II. From Irish word 'Toraidhe' meaning 'cattle thief'. Came to mean any Irish Catholic or Royalist.

First political parties

Whigs and Tories

Who were the Whigs?

They were the first political party in English history.

The party was formed by Shaftesbury who did not want James, a Catholic, to succeed to the throne. They believed that royal powers should be limited and Parliament should be powerful. They wanted the Church to tolerate all Protestants. They conducted peaceful lawful action only. They did not want a regular standing army. They printed a great deal of propaganda to support their views.

Who were the Tories?

They were the political party in opposition to the Whigs.

The Tories supported the Divine Right of Kings and felt that the line of succession should not be interfered with. That is why they supported the King's brother, James, although he was a Catholic. They supported the Church of England and were intolerant of Nonconformists.

The Whigs placed an Exclusion Bill (1679) before Parliament, proposing that James should not be allowed to become King. Charles had a majority in the House of Lords and enough support to defeat the Bill.

Then, in 1682, Shaftesbury plotted an armed rebellion against the King. This was discovered, so he fled abroad. Followers of Shaftesbury decided they would assassinate both Charles and James after a visit to Newmarket races. This plot, known as the Rye Hill plot, was betrayed and several Whig lords were executed.

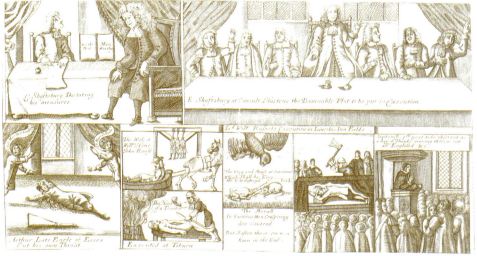

▲ Shaftesbury plotting with fellow Whigs

In 1685 Charles suffered a stroke. As he lay dying, James asked him if he should fetch a Catholic priest. Charles replied, 'For God's sake, brother, do, and lose no time.' Just before his death on February 6, Charles was accepted into the Catholic faith.

Marriage of James to Anne Hyde, Protestant	Birth of Mary, Protestant	Birth of Anne, Protestant	James becomes Catholic	Death of Anne Hyde	Marriage by proxy of James to Mary of Modena, Catholic	Coronation of James II and Mary
1660 September 3	**1662** April 30	**1665** February 6	**1670**	**1671** March 31	**1673** September 30	**1685** April 23

THE FOURTH **18** STUART

James II

James's reign began well in 1685. He promised to 'take care' to defend and support the Church of England. Furthermore, he was a respected army leader and Commander of the Fleet, and he was given customs duties for life. Then he gained esteem for his crushing of a rebellion by the Protestant Duke of Monmouth, the illegitimate son of Charles II.

Monmouth was beheaded after defeat at the Battle of Sedgemoor in July 1685. But James, with the support of Judge Jeffreys, ordered further punishments of Monmouth's supporters. In what became known as the 'Bloody Assizes', Jeffreys, from the safety of the Bench, shouted, swore and laughed at his victims, mostly Nonconformist farm workers.

▲ James II

▲ Judge Jeffreys is seized in 1688 after trying to escape in disguise

Over 300 peasants were hanged, many praising God as they died. It reminded onlookers of the Marian persecution of the 1550s. A further 800 peasants were given to the Queen and her courtiers to sell as slaves to Barbados.

Parliament became alarmed when, after this rebellion, James increased the regulars in his army from 6,000 to 30,000 and formed a Catholic army in Ireland.

Parliament asked James to reduce his army. They also wanted him to dismiss Catholic army officers who, under a Test Act of 1673, were not allowed to hold office. James refused and adjourned Parliament.

He began to use his prerogative to replace Tory ministers with Catholics, dismiss judges, and appoint Catholic bishops and magistrates. He converted two Oxford colleges into places to train Catholic priests and ordered another to take a Catholic president. Within two years he had lost the support of the rich, the poor, political leaders and churchmen.

Seven bishops, one baby

James, having lost the support of the Church of England, now tried to gain some support from the Puritan dissenters.

In 1687 he used his prerogative again and issued a Declaration of Indulgence. This cancelled the Clarendon Code and all other laws against Catholic and Protestant Nonconformists. They could now worship in freedom and take up jobs in the army and government. Thousands of dissenters were released from prison.

In 1688 James issued a Second Declaration of Indulgence and ordered the clergy to read it from their pulpits. Seven bishops, headed by the Archbishop of Canterbury, refused, and petitioned the King.

Why did they do that?

They told the King that the Declaration was against the law since it had not been passed by Parliament.

They claimed the King had no power to change the law on his own. They promised instead to give support for an Act of Toleration which would give Puritans freedom of worship. The Archbishop of Canterbury advised his clergy not to read out this 'illegal' Declaration at their services. Out of 100 London clergy, only four read it. The rest of the clergy in the country decided to support the bishops in defying the King.

Did the King back down?

No, he sent the bishops to trial for sedition.

On the day of the trial, June 29 1688, London was packed. The jury came to a unanimous decision of 'not guilty' and the bishops were acquitted. The city erupted with joy. Bells were rung, bonfires were made, seven candles were lit in windows, portraits engraved and medals struck. The bishops became Protestant heroes throughout the country.

Three weeks before, on June 10, when James's second wife, Mary of Modena, had unexpectedly given birth to a baby boy, James, there had been few celebrations in London.

▲ The seven bishops are taken to the Tower of London

One baby, seven lords

> Were there few celebrations because it meant the next heir to the throne would be Catholic?

> Yes, and one that would replace his step-sisters Mary and Anne, the Protestant daughters of James's first wife, Anne.

▲ The warming-pan baby

James's enemies spread malicious rumours that the baby was a miller's son who had been smuggled into the palace inside a warming-pan.

In this cartoon you can see the over-large baby holding a windmill. Men are looking for evidence that the baby is an impostor while James peeps through the curtains (on the right).

It was the birth of James III, the 'Old Pretender', and the trial of the seven bishops, that finally triggered the revolution of 1688.

Seven Whig and Tory lords combined to write a secret document which invited William of Orange, grandson of Charles I and married to James's daughter Mary, to come to England. He was to come with a military force around which the country could rally against the government of James II.

> Did he accept?

> He did, and risked making such an invasion.

▲ William III in Devon

On November 5, a date which pleased the Protestants, he landed at Brixham in Devon. As his army of 14,000 Protestants from Holland, Belgium, Germany and Scotland marched slowly towards London, so began what became known as the Glorious Revolution.

Glorious and bloodless

Was there much fighting during this Revolution?

Surprisingly, though there were some skirmishes, no blood was shed.

James lost his nerve, his army had lost morale – and he retreated to London, defeated without a battle.

England, therefore, escaped another Civil War. James could have summoned Parliament and stayed on the throne, but he abdicated – choosing to give up the throne himself. On December 11 1688 he stole out of Whitehall but was captured and returned to London. On December 22 he left England for exile in France, never to return.

Was his daughter Mary made Queen?

Mary refused to be Queen unless her husband was King. William, in turn, refused to accept a position as consort under his wife.

Whigs and Tories then united to make them joint sovereigns.

But William and Mary had to agree to certain conditions before accepting the crown. In the same hall of the Banqueting House where Charles I, still believing in the Divine Right of Kings, had stepped out onto the scaffold, William and Mary accepted from the Houses of Lords and Commons the crown, together with a famous Declaration of Rights. From this time on, the Divine Right of Kings to rule was ended in England.

What was truly revolutionary about the Glorious Revolution was that English monarchs no longer had a hereditary claim to the throne to rule with God-given power: they could rule only with Parliament's consent.

▲ A rather extravagant painting showing the triumph of William and Mary (in the middle of the picture, under the canopy). You can see this on a ceiling at the Royal Naval College, Greenwich.

The Revolution settlement

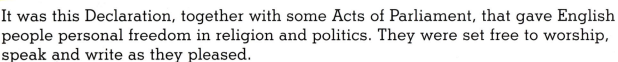

Why was the Declaration of Rights famous?

It marked a turning-point in English and world history.

It was this Declaration, together with some Acts of Parliament, that gave English people personal freedom in religion and politics. They were set free to worship, speak and write as they pleased.

▲ An 18th-century cabinet council

The monarch

After 1688 William, as monarch, still had great power. He had the right to appoint his own cabinet (a small group of Privy Councillors), deal with foreign governments and see to the day-to-day running of the country. Since that time, kings and queens have ruled within the law and with Parliament's agreement. The Glorious Revolution ended the conflict between monarch and Parliament.

Religion

The Declaration stated that the monarch could not be a Roman Catholic or marry a Roman Catholic. Catholics and Unitarians were also excluded from an Act of Toleration (1689). This granted freedom of worship to Protestant Nonconformists, though they were not allowed government or military office, or university education. William, fortunately, did not believe in religious persecution, so Catholics and Unitarians began to be tolerated much more.

The army

The army was still under the orders of William, who chose its officers, but from this time control had to be shared between the monarch and Parliament. Monarchs could only maintain the army by applying every year to Parliament. Never again, in either peace or war, has a monarch been given enough money to keep an army for more than a year. Personal loyalty to the monarch remains the law and tradition of the army today.

Compromise, agreement and toleration

Money

After 1688 the cost of running the country was separated from the cost of funding the monarch. William was given a special payment (Civil List) to cover his personal expenses. The House of Commons held the purse strings of the country and voted on how money was spent. The Bank of England loaned money to the government in return for regular interest payments guaranteed by Parliament. The first 'national debt' became a permanent part of government finances.

Freedom of the press

What is a free press?

A press is free when there is no censorship of it.

▲ The Bank of England is founded in 1694

Only when this is the case can authors and publishers have open discussion on matters such as religion and politics. They can, however, still be tried before a jury for libel. In 1695 the Annual Act for Censorship was allowed to lapse. By 1724 there were 16 newspapers in London alone, besides magazines and journals.

Freedom of speech

From this time on, the House of Commons could speak freely in debate and hold regular elections.

Parliament and law

Parliament became the supreme power in the state. Only it could grant taxes and pass laws. Only it could repeal (cancel) laws. Monarchs could no longer suspend laws, and laws could only be altered by kings, lords and commons together. Judges became independent.

Did all these principles last?

Yes, and they have been adapted and extended to meet the needs of modern democracy as we know it today.

The Daily Courant.

Numb. 2.

Thursday, March 12. 1702.

▲ A front page of the world's first daily newspaper, the Daily Courant

105

Changes in land owned by Catholics (C) and Protestants (P)	P: 41% C: 59%	P: 78% C: 22%	New laws meant Catholics could not:						P: 86% C: 14%
			vote or become MPs	go to university	be lawyers, teachers or soldiers	hold any government jobs	buy land from a Protestant	own horses worth over £5	
Ireland	1641	1688	1690						1703

Ireland and Scotland

William and Mary took the English throne without bloodshed. In Ireland and Scotland it was a different story.

James, no longer king, landed in Ireland in March 1689 with French troops. Catholics rose against Protestants by laying siege to a garrison at Londonderry. The siege lasted six months before being relieved by an English supply ship.

▲ William III at the Battle of the Boyne

William landed in Ireland in June 1690 and on July 1 defeated James's French and Irish army at the Battle of the Boyne. War lasted a year but ended with the Treaty of Limerick in 1691.

William wanted religious freedom for the Irish but was overruled by the Dublin Parliament. New laws succeeded in suppressing the Irish leaders, the gentry and the educated.

By 1703, though greatly outnumbered by the Catholics, Protestants owned most of the land. The conquest of Ireland was complete.

What happened in Scotland?

After the Revolution, the Presbyterian Kirk became the official Church and bishops were abolished. The mainly Protestant lowlanders accepted this but the Catholic highlanders rebelled. After a victory at Killicrankie in July 1689, the rebels were defeated by the Protestant Covenanters at Dunkeld.

After this, the highland clans agreed to take an oath of loyalty to William by January 1 1692. The chief of the MacDonald clan of Glencoe missed the deadline and the Edinburgh government ordered punishment. After staying as guests of the MacDonalds, 100 troops led by a captain of the rival Campell clan massacred 38 of the MacDonalds.

By 1700 bad harvests and famine affected Scotland. Their merchants were prevented from trading on their own by the English, whose own merchants were making huge profits from colonial trade.

England and Wales	Scotland	Ireland	British settlers overseas	Total: 13.75 million
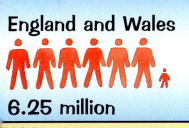 6.25 million	 1.25 million	 3.25 million	3 million	

750 Population estimates

Changes

In 1485, when Henry VII became the first Tudor monarch, England was, by and large, an insignificant nation with no colonies. Foreign ambassadors visiting England had learnt Spanish, French and Italian for diplomatic purposes, but never bothered to learn English.

By 1700, however, the English language was spreading worldwide. English colonies helped to establish the language as, by this time, England had become the centre of a thriving colonial empire.

The unglamorous import Canadian cod had been joined by exotic Indian silk, jewels, porcelain, ivory and tea, and by American coffee, sugar and tobacco.

London was the largest city in Europe and its city was at the heart of a worldwide trade.

The Bank of England and other banks made it easier for merchants to borrow and pay back money. People could buy shares in trading companies from stockbrokers. Insurance companies covered losses.

Merchants formed joint stock companies which shared ships, warehouses, agents and defences against pirates. They made huge profits for their shareholders from the sale all over Europe of raw materials from Canada, America and India.

The companies' ships not only brought raw materials from all over the world to England, they exported manufactured goods made from those materials. From this time on, the rise and fall in the power of European nations was often closely tied to their trade and empires overseas.

This was certainly the case for Britain in the following 200 years.

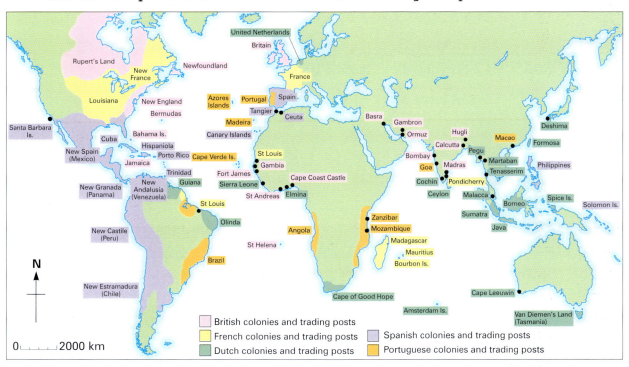

▲ Colonies of European nations in about 1700. The world was linked by the ships of these nations.

107

Kings and queens of England and Ireland

Name	Also known as	Age at succession	Family	Died	Buried
Henry VII	First King of the House of Tudor	Age 28 as King of England and Lord of Ireland	Wife: Elizabeth of York Children: Arthur, Margaret, HENRY, Elizabeth, Mary, Edward, Catherine	April 5, Richmond Age 52 Of gout and pneumonia	Westminster Abbey
Born 1457		♛ 1485		**Died 1509**	
Henry VIII	Bluff King Hal (in retrospect)	Age 17 as King of England and Lord of Ireland. Styled himself King of Ireland from 1544	Wife 1: Catherine of Aragon 2: Anne Boleyn 3: Jane Seymour 4: Anne of Cleves 5: Katherine Howard 6: Catherine Parr Children of Catherine of Aragon: MARY Children of Anne Boleyn: ELIZABETH Children of Jane Seymour: EDWARD	January 28, Westminster Age 55 Of kidney disease, gout and a circulatory disorder made worse by a leg ulcer	Windsor
Born 1491		♛ 1509		**Died 1547**	
Edward VI		Age 9 as King of England and Ireland	Unmarried	July 6, Greenwich Age 15 Of tuberculosis	King Henry VII's Chapel, Westminster Abbey
Born 1537		♛ 1547		**Died 1553**	
Jane	Nine Days' Queen	Age 16 proclaimed secretly as Queen of England and Ireland	Husband: Lord Guildford Dudley Children: None	February 12, Tower of London Age 16 Executed by beheading	St Peter-ad-Vincula, Tower of London, between remains of Anne Boleyn and Katherine Howard
Born 1537		♛ 1553		**Died 1554**	
Mary	Bloody Mary	Age 37 as Queen of England and Ireland	Husband: Philip II (King of Spain) Children: None	November 17, St James's Palace Age 42 Of pneumonia after a history of illness including dropsy	King Henry VII's Chapel, Westminster Abbey
Born 1516		♛ 1553		**Died 1558**	

Kings and queens of England, Ireland and Scotland

Name	Also known as	Age at succession	Family	Died	Buried
Elizabeth I Born 1533	The Virgin Queen Gloriana	Age 25 as Queen of England and Ireland 👑 1558	Unmarried	March 24, Richmond Age 69 Of old age and pneumonia following a chill **Died 1603**	King Henry VII's Chapel, Westminster Abbey
James I (James VI of Scotland) Born 1566		Age 13 months as King James VI of Scotland Age 36 as King James I of England and Ireland 👑 1603	Wife: Anne of Denmark Children: Henry, Frederick, Elizabeth, Margaret, CHARLES, Robert, Mary, Sophia	March 27, Theobalds, Hertfordshire Age 58 Of premature old age and fever with paroxysms following a chill **Died 1625**	King Henry VII's Chapel, Westminster Abbey
Charles I Born 1600	Charles, King and Martyr (after his death)	Age 24 as King of England, Scotland and Ireland 👑 1625	Wife: Henrietta Maria Children: Charles (died), CHARLES, Mary, JAMES, Elizabeth, Anne, Catherine, Henry, Henrietta, Anne	January 30, Whitehall Age 49 Executed by beheading **Died 1649**	Windsor
Charles II Born 1630		Age 19 as King of England, Scotland and Ireland 👑 1660	Wife: Catherine of Braganza Children: None legitimate	February 6, Whitehall Age 54 Of a stroke **Died 1685**	Westminster Abbey
James II Born 1633		Age 51 as King of England, Scotland and Ireland 👑 1685	Wife 1: Anne Hyde 2: (By proxy) Maria Beatrice d'Este (Mary of Modena) Children of Anne: Charles, MARY, James, ANNE, Charles, Edgar, Henrietta, Catherine Children of Mary: Catherine, Isabella, Charles, Elizabeth, Charlotte, JAMES, Louisa	September 6, St Germain, France Age 67 Of a paralytic stroke **Died 1701**	St Germain Body disappeared during French Revolution
William III Born 1650	Prince of Orange (before his succession)	Age 39 as King of England and Ireland on February 23 and as King of Scotland on May 11 👑 1689	Wife: Mary Children: None	March 8, Kensington Palace Age 51 Of a broken collarbone sustained when his horse stumbled over a molehill **Died 1702**	Westminster Abbey
and Mary II Born 1662		Age 26 as Queen of England and Ireland on February 23 and as Queen of Scotland on May 11 👑 1689	Husband: William Children: None	December 28, Kensington Palace Age 32 Of smallpox **Died 1694**	King Henry VII's Chapel, Westminster Abbey

Kings and queens of Scotland

Name	Also known as	Age at succession	Family	Died	Buried
James IV		Age 15 as King of Scotland	Wife: Margaret Tudor Children: James (died), daughter who died after baptism, Arthur, JAMES, unnamed daughter, Alexander	September 9, Flodden, Northumberland Age 40 In battle	Above ground at monastery at Sheen, Richmond, Surrey Body removed to Church of St Michael, City of London
Born 1473		👑 1488		**Died 1513**	
James V	Poor Man's King	Age 17 months as King of Scotland	Wife 1: Madeleine de Valois 2: Marie de Guise Lorraine Children of Marie: James, Arthur, MARY	December 14, Falkland Age 30 Of melancholia	Holyrood Abbey Body taken during Glorious Revolution, destiny unknown
Born 1512		👑 1513		**Died 1542**	
Mary Queen of Scots		Age about 7 days as Queen of Scotland	Husband 1: Francois, Dauphin of France 2: Henry Stewart, Lord Darnley 3: James Hepburn, Earl of Bothwell and Duke of Orkney Children of Darnley: JAMES	February 8, Fotheringay Castle, Northants Age 44 Executed by beheading	Peterborough Cathedral Body removed to King Henry VII's Chapel, Westminster Abbey
Born 1542		👑 1542		**Died 1587**	
James VI (James I of England)		See Kings of England, Ireland and Scotland			
Born 1566					

Index